The Coming Age Revolution

The Coming Age Revolution

(when growing old will be great)

by Reginald Stackhouse

The Coming Age Revolution
Copyright ©2005 by Reginald Stackhouse

We acknowledge the financial support of the Government of Canada through the Book Publishing Industry Development Program for our publishing activities.

ISBN: 1-894622-66-9

Published by Warwick Publishing Inc.
161 Frederick Street, Suite 200
Toronto, Ontario M5A 4P3 Canada
www.warwickgp.com

Distributed in Canada by
Canadian Book Network
c/o Georgetown Terminal Warehouses
34 Armstrong Avenue
Georgetown, Ontario L7G 4R9

Distributed in the United States by
CDS
193 Edwards Drive
Jackson TN 38301
www.cdsbooks.com

Design: Clint Rogerson

Printed and bound in Canada

TO MARGARET

Bride of my youth
Companion of my age
Partner of all the years in between

I have travelled the land,
I have seen the world,
I have heard it all.

The questions of my childhood
I have answered.

The things I have dreamed of
I have done.

But when I look
Into the eyes of an elder,
I have not done enough.

Lincoln Tutt
Arctic Village, Alaska, 1993

Contents

Preface

When you think of revolutions, what picture comes into your mind? It may be sinister-looking people who meet behind locked doors and plan terrorist attacks. But here is a story about another kind of revolution. A happy kind. A peaceful kind.

In the 1984 election campaign for president of the United States, the Republican campaign committee was worried. Their candidate had just finished an effective four years as president. He was one of the most popular men to have been in the White House. But his committee was still worried. They feared one thing might sink him.

At 73, Ronald Reagan's age might reduce his ability to out-campaign his 56-year-old opponent, Walter Mondale. They also feared the public might give way to a built-in bias against hiring older people.

They didn't need to worry. Their candidate had already worked out how he would handle the age question. He wanted his opposition to go public with it. He was really lying in wait when a journalist challenged him, in the first TV debate of the campaign, to say if he thought age might be an issue in the election.

"Yes," Reagan answered, "I have thought so. And I am resolved not to use my opponent's youth and inexperience against him." This brilliant and totally unexpected retort brought the house down. Even Mondale had to laugh. Most important, it drew cheers and laughs right across the country. After that, no one mentioned President Reagan's 73 years of age again. He won by a landslide. But it was more than an election victory.

As a song once put it, this was "the start of something big." In a country that had always been fascinated by youth and novelty, a septuagenarian had shown he could win the White House. He could become the oldest president ever re-elected. But his victory means more than even that.

The calendar could no longer dictate how people would have to live. The coming of an age revolution had been announced.

Acknowledgments

My thanks must go to the many people and institutions that have made this book possible:

My wife, Margaret, read the entire manuscript and gave me the benefit of her insights.

The libraries of the University of Toronto, the Toronto School of Theology, the John Graham Library, the Toronto Reference Library, the Deer Park Public Library, and the Canadian Centre for Philanthropy were all sources of useful material. Their staffs were uniformly courteous and resourceful.

Since this is not an academic book, I have not often used quotations, footnotes or other references to acknowledge the material drawn from a large number of sources. All of them, however, have been named in the Bibliography at the end of the book.

My thanks go to the writers who have contributed so ably to this subject area.

It has been a pleasure to work with Nick Pitt, president of Warwick Publishing, Toronto, and his editorial colleagues in producing this book.

Chapter 1

Winds of Change

"Elders of the world unite, you have nothing to lose but your canes."

A social prophet today could issue this kind of statement, echoing Marx and Engels in 1848 when they asked the workers of the world to unite (and lose their chains). But none really needs to. The 21st century has begun with irrefutable signs of a coming age revolution that are clear for all to see.

This revolution will be different from others the world has seen, be they political or social. It will not be accompanied by suicide bombers or vocal protesters filling city squares. It is not being shaped by a cabal of sinister conspirators plotting in backrooms. This revolution is starting with all the men and women — some of them famous, most not — who are demonstrating how growing older does not have to mean quitting, or even slowing down, or anything like withdrawing from the world and letting it pass them by.

That's why someone like world-class writer Alice Munro (b. 1931) is not only still writing into her seventies but is winning awards that other writers — decades younger — can only dream of. Her readers know, of course, that doing the unexpected is her style. Where other writers have assumed their genius could be fulfilled only in a glamorous metropolis — a New York or a Paris — Munro has expressed her genius in and through small-town Ontario. A less glamorous, less exciting setting would be hard to find, yet her stories are read by hundreds of thousands of avid fans around the world. Her fame and her stunning literary output have only increased as she grows older.

That's the message of the coming age revolution. To grow older does not have to mean becoming marginalized.

Even in the executive suite — that fortress of convention — where it has been assumed that a person should expect to leave gracefully and affluently by a mandatory age, there are examples of people who are unwilling to go to the sidelines. Sumner Redstone (b. 1921) has remained at the top of the entertainment industry even though he is an octogenarian. If we assume it is good business to leave business in the hands of those under the age of 60, how do we explain this man who heads up Viacom, the conglomerate that includes Columbia Broadcasting, Paramount Pictures, Simon & Schuster Publishing, as well as 14 other entertainment companies? And this is not all that Sumner Redstone is responsible for: he also presides over National Amusements, which operates 1,400 motion picture theatres across the United States. Is it any wonder that many see him as the top media mogul in an industry crowded with moguls?

In one's 80s, convention dictates rest, relaxation, and declining health, but this has not occurred to Sumner Redstone. In addition to running his corporate empire he is also actively involved in community service — philanthropies, hospitals, universities — as both a donor and supporter.

Why does he do it? The answer is revolutionary to people who assume we change radically once we pass an invisible time line. In his 80s Redstone is essentially the person he was in his youth, someone with a "passion to win" (the title of his autobiography that he penned at 77), a passion he says his mother instilled in him, a passion demonstrated by his immigrant father who made a living as a linoleum salesman, both parents seeing to it that their overachieving son received the best education available. There is a message about aging in all this.

We can be in age what we were in youth. Some of us may slow down, but none of us need give up. This social change will make the 21st century a new age for aging.

It's not easy to think of a revolution when the name of a billionaire is mentioned in conjunction to it. But on Canada's west coast, that is what James Pattison (b. 1928) represents, not only because he flies in the face of conventional business wisdom by still operating a conglomerate in eight distinctive commercial areas. Nor because he holds personal sway over this empire despite its demanding that he be on the job each day — ready to fly around the country to close deals far from his Vancouver base. But because Jimmy, as he is widely known, could be thought too old for this kind of thing, too old for anything but memories of action. He is into the fourth quarter of life's game, which is enough to disqualify him from most jobs. And that's why he represents a revolution — the new wave of the 21st century that will carry people long past what was so recently thought of as quitting time.

What's more, Jimmy is making a fresh impact on the world of business. So much so that he has been given new international recognition by being granted the Horatio Alger Award (two previous recipients were Billy Graham and Oprah Winfrey) — a mountain-sized achievement for anyone, anywhere, but all the more impressive for someone who started as a car salesman in a country with only the 30th-largest population in the world. Even more, it's because he could win that prestigious award as a septuagenarian that Jimmy represents a future for which history shows no precedent.

A social revolution is gathering force in all countries where the same dynamics are at work to make the 21st century a new age for aging. It is already changing life for older people. It will change life even more for men and women moving past middle age in the next 20 years.

Like other upheavals at this stage, it seems no larger than a cloud on the horizon. But even one cloud can herald a coming storm. It may be only an incipient force now, but this storm will become strong enough to radicalize the world's assumptions about aging in the 21st century. It's going to be different to grow older. It's going to be better.

What the gender and race revolutions did to change the 20th century, the age revolution will do in the 21st. Already, the winds of change are blowing hard enough for today's elders to recognize they should not assume that things must remain as they have been. But they are not the only people of the age revolution. The Boomer Generation that did so much to alter society in their youth will be its epicenter. They will be the Number One dynamic for change in this century.

From ancient times to modern, aging has meant enough deprivation and marginalization that most people can appreciate Winston Churchill's saying, "Everybody wants to go on living, but nobody wants to grow old." Why would we?

In the past growing older has meant losing health, strength and mobility for many, or losing work, income and independence for others. Nor has that been all. Aging has meant being pushed to the sidelines as spectators instead of being on the field as participants. The march of time has meant life's clouding over.

Nothing short of an age revolution will change this. That's the right word for it. Not all revolutions are political upheavals with riots in the streets that lead to rulers being turned out of their palaces.

The word "revolution" was first used by the astronomer, Nicholas Copernicus (1473–1543) for the title of his pattern-setting work, *The Book of Revolutions*. But he intended it just to describe the way the planets revolved around the sun.

It first took on a political meaning over a century later when the British parliament, having driven James II from the throne, called this upheaval "a glorious revolution." But it would expand to a still wider meaning in the centuries ahead.

It would be applied to social changes radical enough to go down to the roots of a culture, tear them up and sow new seeds to start all over again. Such as the earth-moving impact on industry made by James Watt's (1736–1819) invention of the steam engine, an impact great enough that it could be called the Industrial Revolution.

Didn't we see the same kind of revolution in the 20th century too? In the democratic West, radical social changes transformed the daily culture in which ordinary people lived, moved and had their being.

When Rosa Parks sat down in the white section of a Birmingham, Alabama bus because at the end of a 1955 work day, she was too tired to stand, she triggered nothing short of a revolution in American race relations. Not only would it make her free to sit on any seat in any bus of any city in the United States, but the race revolution would open public offices so that members of her race could sit on the Supreme Court, become chair of the joint chiefs of staff, Secretary of State, or be elected sheriffs in southern counties where white officers had once tyrannized blacks with fire hoses and police dogs.

Something just as radical happened to gender relations too. Betty Friedan (b. 1921) may not have known that her 1963 book, The Feminine Mystique, would be the match to set off a powder keg of demand for change regarding the status of women. But it was. And by the end of the century, women could become CEOs in major corporations, hold combat roles in the military, become half or more of the student body in professional schools, and form a major part of the work force. Women would still be feminine. But the feminine mystique would be no more.

Now people are about to see the end of another set of prejudices. It's called *ageism.*

It will end not because of protest marches on the seats of power. Nor because of an ideological critique formed in an academic study, and still less because of a reformist initiative in a political assembly. Aging in the 21st century will be different because the numbers will be different. The force for change will be a simple, bloodless, unimaginative matter of demographics. Not barricades in city squares. Just figures in the census telling us the time for change has come to people who are aging.

Older people are living longer and staying healthier. On the other side of the equation, fewer younger people are being born. Add those two statistical facts together and the sum is enough to revolutionize the role older people will play in 21st century society. In the past, demographics could be illustrated by a pyramid because there were relatively fewer elders at the top and a very large number of younger people at the base. Not so now, not so in the future. The pyramid has not yet been completely inverted. But that is conceivable. Already it is taking on the pear shape it will soon have when the middle becomes larger than the bottom. The death rate and the birth rate are already too small for North American demographics to look as they did at mid-20th century. Something has to give. It will be our assumptions about aging. Demographics are dictating it.

In the United States, the number of men and women 65 years of age and over was 25,555,000 in 1980. Just 20 years later, it had escalated to 34,992,000. A 35% increase! But that's not the end. If current trends continue, the number of Americans 65 and over will be double the number still in their teens. Only in America, you ask? To make the future demographic impact still more powerful, the same trend is running throughout the developed world.

Across the European Union, the number of people 65 or more had jumped to 17% of the population in 2001. Canadians anticipate that by 2015, there will be as many people 65 years or over as there will be children under 16. In Australia, the 65-plus population had leaped to 18.3% of the population by 2001.

If we look at Asia, we find the same trend rushing forward like a car in the Grand Prix. Where the number of Japanese aged 60 or more was 22.1% of the national population in 1998, it is expected to be 33% by 2025.

The elder population in the city-state of Singapore will catapult from 9.9% to 28.1%. South Korea's from 10.1 to 23.4%. Thailand's from 9.3% to 20.1%. Massive China's from 9.9% to 19.9%. Except for the Middle East, Africa and parts of Latin America, the world will grow gray.

Understandably, prophecies about inverting the demographic pyramid have alarmed people who now fear that if their country is becoming a kind of national retirement home, who will keep them going? The possibilities become enough to make people manic and depressive at the same time. They are told their pension funds may default because there will not be enough young workers to sustain them. The "graying of America" was so advanced by the start of the 21st century that Federal Reserve Board Chairman Alan Greenspan warned that it could make "Social Security and Medicare programs unsustainable." Private pension funds were in such jeopardy in 2003 that a report by Watson Wyatt claimed it would take $1.5 trillion over the next five years to make up the shortfall — if employing companies made adequate contributions. But it could take 18 years if employers did not.

Yet the future viability of their pension funds is not the only concern of today's citizens. They wonder what the future holds at the international level when they picture massive armies of foreign young people threatening a country if it has to rely on old people to shoulder arms.

They ask who will keep the economy moving when there may not be enough young people to do the heavy lifting, and so on, until the future seems an enemy to dread, not a friend to welcome.

But those fears are based on the assumption that nothing about older people needs to change, that they must remain in their marginalized and dependent way of life. That the older population's growth must inexorably be a problem rather than an opportunity.

What people need to grasp is how each of those hazards can be contained when older people reverse the direction in which tradition has pointed them. That is why the age revolution has to come. It can make everyone a winner. Young and old alike.

Through the centuries, humanity has survived and prospered by using an incredible genius for adaptation. We are going to see that genius at work again. How? By shaping a new revolution with characteristics found in every social development that has succeeded.

FROM BELOW

It will not be initiated at the top. No revolution has been. None can be. So no one should expect this new phenomenon will result from legislation, although it will involve a revolutionary impact on existing statutes. Our laws and institutions represent the old ageist culture that has to go. And will go. Change must be sought from below.

When Martin Luther King led the fight for racial justice in America, he succeeded because he focused his leadership on the people that were with him as much as he directed his message against officials and employers oppressing his people. He could not have been more prudent. Even a superstar cannot be a leader without followers. So in Birmingham, Alabama, Rosa Parks had to be joined by thousands of men and women who would walk to work day after day rather than board segregated buses. But that was not all.

King had to inspire the common people night after night at their prayer meetings because the race revolution could take its great leap forward only if they would stay the course. Success at the top depended on determination at the bottom. The rank and file had to sustain their courage in the face of violent threats. They had to control their desire to lash back in a violent reaction that would have been futile. So

King focused on the bottom, where ultimately every revolution wins or fails.

The age revolution will advance because of people who recognize that they do not have to cling to their assumptions about age and its limitations. No revelation from on high. No heavily financed study commission. No new government project. Just men and women convincing themselves and others they still have a job to do.

That can be no easy turnaround because so much of our culture reinforces the old order. French men and women thus have to contend with a long advocated division of time into three ages: Preparation (youth); Production (maturity); and the Third Age (the years when we can fulfill ourselves as persons). It is an inviting concept which has obvious appeal. In the midst of those busy, harassed, stressed out production years, what mature donkey would not be attracted by the carrot of that Third Age?

In North America, that carrot has been waved in front of people as "Freedom 55" — the chance to drop out of the rat race at age 55. Then enjoy the rest of life with a guaranteed income. Beautiful! Seductive! Even productive! At least for the retirement industry with its golf courses, gated communities, cruise lines, and gambling casinos.

The age revolution's countervailing force will be older people rethinking their role in the world.

The great social revolutions of the 20th century did not come about because one or more political parties took up the cause of women and the rights of racial minorities, but these radical changes did involve organizations like the National Association for Women, the National Association for the Advancement of Colored People, the Southern Christian Leadership Conference, and the Congress of Racial Equality. Yes, these organizations were all pressing for legislative reforms. But they were not the genius of the struggle. The genius was in people finding new ways to understand themselves. That process was imperative if a society was to transform itself for the better.

Before World War II, a black man could feel lucky if he landed a job as a Pullman car porter on a train. It was steady work. Clean work. Well paid (for those times). But one thing was sure. A black man could not be anything else on a train. Not a conductor. Not an engineer.

Nothing. Just a porter. Only when Canadians and Americans of African ancestry started to redefine themselves could they think of careers that involved something different from carrying other people's luggage and making up their berths.

Something like becoming the Queen's representative in Ontario, Canada's largest province, or before that, Canada's Minister of Labour. What son of a train porter could have ambitions like those? Lincoln Alexander could and did.

He put himself through university, then became a lawyer, and next won election after election as the invincible M.P. for a constituency in the industrial city of Hamilton. But none of it would have happened if "Link" (as everyone called him) had not first thought new thoughts about himself. Thoughts his forbears could not think. And because he could think them, he could do his part in making a race revolution a great new fact of his time.

History itself shows that thinking new thoughts about ourselves is the first step in any revolution. But not just about ourselves, a revolution cannot burst on the world unless people have started to look differently at the world itself.

NEW CONCEPTS

Before any of the great political upheavals of history could be activated, new ideas had to be articulated and circulated. The American Revolution could not have succeeded if it had depended solely on Washington and the Congressional Army. It needed people reading a book that became the 18th century's best seller — Tom Paine's *Common Sense* (1776). Its message showed how the War of Independence could mean more than a change of government in what had been 13 colonies. It could mean a new humanity.

It was vital for Thomas Jefferson and other political leaders to correspond with each other about the kind of country they wanted to emerge from the struggle. But an intellectual turnaround was needed below them before there could be people for them to lead. Americans had to conceive themselves differently than any people had before them. For their leaders to fashion a new nation at the top, these leaders had to rely on common people jettisoning centuries of assumptions that power should belong to a superior elite. They had to become men and women who could believe government depended on the consent of the governed. We have become so used to thinking that way that we forget what a radical, innovative, revolutionary concept it was. But without it, the leaders of the 13 colonies could have found themselves without the support needed to sustain five years of war against a great power.

So the coming age revolution depends on 21st-century elders renewing their minds and thinking new thoughts about themselves and their place in the world as they advance in years. It will come about through people such as Walter Cronkite who, despite retiring as anchor man for *CBS Evening News* in 1981, still puts in an eight- to ten-hour day of interviews, articles, TV documentaries, and books, as well as going on the lecture circuit. "The most trusted man in America," as he was called in his nightly news broadcasting days, rejects the assumption that in his 80s, a person has nothing much to give the world. And that is more significant than it may seem. Revolutions begin when people have the courage to think new thoughts about themselves.

The demand for women's equality could not have found voices and votes in the 20th century without some women moving beyond the assumptions of their culture. They had to redefine what a woman's place in society was. They could be denied leadership roles only as long as they too agreed that, when it came to running a business, governing a country, or practicing a profession, they were not as capable as men.

Similarly, African-Americans could not rise above the level to which the white majority confined them until they convinced one another that they were not inferior by nature. They just had had inferior opportunities. They needed to rethink what it meant to be black. That was why asserting "Black Is Beautiful" was more than an aesthetic statement. It signaled a reversal of all the self-immolation that blacks had to make on the altar of white supremacy. It meant the blacks of America could rise because they had raised themselves in their own eyes. But to develop such new concepts requires something else that's new.

NEW WORDS

It is a new language. Every revolution has demanded that people shake off the vocabulary that was keeping the old order in place. That was why the noble eloquence of the Declaration of Independence about the right to "life, liberty and the pursuit of happiness" was clutched at by Americans. And why the French Revolution could rally around "Liberty, Equality, and Fraternity." Those words were not just slogans. They gave people the linguistic tools with which to fashion a new self-consciousness.

That was also why, in the 20th century, women's liberation demanded our dropping sexist terms and humor that reinforced traditional biases. This was no optional demand. One way our culture now shows it has changed is the way sexist language is no longer acceptable.

The race revolution also meant a language cleansing. All the terms and labels that had upheld a master race/inferior race social dichotomy had to be washed out of usage.

Political correctness may seem nit-picking to many, but a society cannot have major change if it still uses language that implies there wasn't any change at all.

An age revolution demands impact on our vocabulary if we are to start to think differently about aging. Thoughts without words are impossible because thinking is no more than a silent conversation with oneself. To think new thoughts about ourselves as we grow older will therefore be expedited as we gain a new language about aging.

Out will go not only the obviously offensive terms like "geezer," "fuddy-duddy," "little old lady," "old man," "pops." So will go seemingly inoffensive terms like "retirement" and "senior citizen," even though these euphemisms are intended to avoid giving offence. Why? Because of the next characteristic that this social revolution will demand.

LINES OF DEMARCATION

The age revolution will erase the lines of demarcation that have marginalized older people, gently but irresistibly pushing them to the edge and beyond. Revolutions always have that impact on a society. The American Revolution thus produced a society whose constitution purported to assure all citizens the same rights. The French Revolution removed all aristocratic titles because they separated a small elite from the common mass in a country that now affirmed the equality of all. Instead of a few being called "M. le duc" or M. le comte," everyone was called "Citizen." In 1917, the Russian Revolution led to everyone being called "Comrade." The Communist Revolution in China clothed everyone in the same civilian "uniform" so that the old divide between rich elite and impoverished mass would be swept away.

True, revolutions have often produced new lines of demarcation. But only after removing the old ones. The coming age revolution will do no less. It will not accept people assuming that at a certain point in time they move into a new social classification that distinguishes them from younger and more productive men and women. A common humanity will be accepted, one that is not fragmented by persons reaching that age.

Focus groups composed of people 65 or more organized by the Seniors Secretariat of Health and Welfare Canada revealed a common dislike of the designation, "senior citizen." To the focus group participants, it suggested frail, very old people, the kind of person the focus group members did not want to be considered. But that was not all.

This response also suggested that Canadians 65 and over were rejecting old concepts about themselves and reaching out for new ones. They were starting to think revolutionary thoughts about their society and their place in it.

Similarly, the gender and race revolutions both put a high price on opening institutions and positions that had been closed to them. For a men's organization to become open to women, or a senior government office be given to an African-American meant more than access. It meant that the old barriers were coming down, and that the common humanity of everyone was being accepted.

That was why it mattered to see the 21st century start with Hillary Clinton entering the Senate on her own instead of at her presidential husband's side, Colin Powell representing the United States to the world as secretary of state, and Condoleezza Rice symbolizing both revolutions as a black, woman Ph.D. who had earned her place in the White House as United States president George W. Bush's security advisor and then successor to Powell as secretary of state.

The whole human rights movement is based on that conviction because it affirms rights that demand no qualification from people other than that they are human. Where those rights are concerned, there are no lines demarking those humans who enjoy them and those who are denied them. If they are human, they are qualified. Basic to the age revolution will be the same commitment to our common humanity. No lines will separate us from one another because some are older, some younger.

In his 1999 "Letter to the Elderly," Pope John Paul II cited Cicero, the ancient Roman orator, who wrote: "The burden of age is lighter for those who feel respected and loved by the young." That is achieved best when a revolution breaks down the walls that have shut people out from easy association with each other. Some larger-than-life men and women can do that all on their own.

As a young man, Ted Turner worked for his father's advertising firm. Even then he was always driving himself in the "flat out" style the public would later associate with him after he built CNN, married Jane Fonda, and bought the Atlanta Braves. But his work ethic did not stop when he became older. He could still sell CNN after making himself a five-star celebrity, defend the America's Cup, merge AOL with Time/Warner, and lead environmentalist crusades. He might have been older but he could not just stop working.

At an age when, free from financial constraints, people are assumed to want unlimited leisure and pleasure, Turner started up a new business. Not television news services this time, but fast food restaurants, Ted's Montana Grill. He also amassed the largest bison herd in the world at an age when everyone was supposed to retire. Yet what does that prove about the majority of men and women?

Just because a superman like Turner erases the line between old and young, retired and active, what does that tell us about the rest of the human race who are just plain folks? It reminds us that revolutions are always heralded by individuals prescient enough to look further into the future than most people see.

In the 20th century, we saw that happen with race and gender. But will it be possible with age now? Are there not facts of nature that force us to see that while we are all human, some of us are less human than others?

The barriers blocking the advance of the age revolution are not facts but myths, unsupported prejudices about aging that have to be shown for what they are. Before the American Civil War, it was acknowledged by thinking southerners that slavery could be accepted only if blacks really were inferior to whites. Otherwise it would be intolerable for one human to purport having ownership of another human. That was in the 19th century, but not just then.

To continue segregating the races into the 20th century depended on white supremacists maintaining a mythology of race. The race revolution succeeded only after that mythology was successfully challenged. The gender revolution was the same. It could happen only when knowledge replaced assumption.

Now it has to happen again.

The coming age revolution is beginning in the same place that all great revolutions have begun: by demythologizing the past.

Chapter 2

Demythologizing Age

Religious myths are part of antiquity, but secular myths are part of modernity. They lack supernatural beings, but they elevate normal people to a superhuman level. That's why they pack such power in their psychological impact.

Almost every nation sustains its people's pride with myths about its unique heroism, virtue and mission, which are shared in stories about larger-than-life persons. Their importance cannot be exaggerated because their hold on the popular imagination has persisted through history. And their power for incarcerating our minds in psychological prisons should not be minimized. Especially when we see how older people are so often "cribbed, cabined and confined" by the age myths our culture takes for granted.

Every static social structure has been held in place by a mythology. Kings once ruled by a myth that they had a divine right to power. Aristocrats enjoyed privileges based on a myth that they were better than their subjects because they were the products of nobler "breeding." White supremacy depended on a myth that white people were inherently superior to every other race in intelligence and character. Male dominance needed the myth that women were incapable of functioning on an equal basis with men.

Each of those power structures could crash down only when their mythical foundations were laid bare by the tides of critical protest. As long as they were believed, people were ready to accept servitude as though the arrangement were part of nature itself. Once the myths were challenged though, liberation became possible. That is where the threat to ageism lies now as the 21st century begins. For the first time, a serious challenge can be raised against age mythology. And it has to be taken seriously.

Only this challenge can free people from the inner, psychological bondage of myths that have kept older people in invisible but no less constricting shackles. One of them is based on the same assumption all profiling requires to be believed.

"THEY'RE ALL ALIKE"

Like sexism and racism, ageism depends on people being prejudged by stereotyping them. Before the gender and race revolutions of the 20th century, women and people of color could be held down by being viewed strictly in terms of unsubstantiated and negative generalizations about them. In the 21st century, it is still possible to assume that whatever is true about one older person must be applicable to all the others.

This kind of thinking is as vital to ageism as it was to the racism which made this kind of police incident possible. When a Toronto convenience store was held up, the fleeing robber was tackled by a citizen who held the armed thief tight while the merchant called the police. On arriving and seeing a white man and a black man, the two police officers immediately grabbed the black with the intent of hustling him off to the station house for questioning.

Fortunately the merchant shouted: "Not him. The other guy." It was just in time. So convinced had the officers been that blacks were more prone to thievery than whites that these policemen went where a "they're all alike" mythology led them.

Older people know what it means to be prejudged that way too — by no other criterion than their calendar age. Any student in Logic IA learns that generalizations are generally wrong. But people past a certain age know they are facing a brick wall of discrimination when they are looking for work. So some fake the dates on their résumés. Or leave them off altogether. Many dye their hair. Others resort to cosmetic surgery. All these measures are deemed essential to getting a job when ageism is a negative but powerful factor. The mythology that anyone older than a predetermined age is less capable than anyone below that age is just too much for them to overcome. Myth trumps reason. And the results can be tragic.

History shows how ageism robs society of some of its greatest human resources today. In its heyday, when Venice was the financial and trading center of Europe, its citizens seldom elected anyone under 50 to the city-state's governing body, and no one became the Doge who was below 60. Even more, the medieval Church knew the price of age discrimination was a high one, and it did not bow to the calendar's dictate. Lanfranc (1005–89) was 65 when he became Archbishop of Canterbury and stayed in office until age 84. Why is it so hard for us to liberate ourselves now from myths about older workers? Especially when we open our eyes to what is a whitecap on the horizon now — but will be the wave of the future.

In Ottawa, Canada's capital city, on any business day for many years, people could notice a 92-year-old on his way to work. Former cabinet minister Mitchell Sharpe (1912–2004) was still doing his bit in the government of Canada. He was a personal advisor to the prime minister, Jean Chrétien, who had started his rise to the top job by being made a parliamentary secretary to Sharpe, then the minister of finance. The two men clicked and stayed so *en rapport* that when Chrétien needed some personal counsel, he sent for his old boss, this time at a dollar-a-year so that the pensioned former minister would not be criticized for "double dipping."

Chrétien's own retirement meant the end of the job for Sharpe too, but not yet the end of the road. He was approached right away by two public officials not prejudiced against having a 92-year-old on their staffs when he knew about government as much as Sharpe did — and even more, knew as much about human nature. Only mythology restricts our view of that common sense attribute as being something rare.

Employers can be reminded that there are big differences among people of the same age group. Most of all, they will struggle over accepting the reality that there are as many individual differences among older people as among younger. Why is it so difficult for them to judge older applicants just on their individual merits? So difficult for employers to grasp that older people are like anyone else, just older?

The individuality that marked applicants when they were younger does not vanish when people become older, but that fact is hard to grasp when one thinks mythologically. It infects our minds even when we want to give someone a compliment. When others say, "But you don't seem old!" they reflect this myth even though it does not fit reality.

Apart from physical changes, men and women in their older years remain much the same persons they were in youth. Some traits may become more accentuated but the core personality usually continues. As well, older people — like younger people — remain distinct from each other in all the abilities, interests, attitudes, and everything else that made them unique when they were younger.

Former president George Bush (b. 1924) parachuted from a plane at age 75 to show (as he told reporters) "old guys can still do stuff." And he did it again at age 80. In doing so, Bush proved that age had not changed him as a person. In his inner self, he was still the man who could survive being shot down in World War II as a U.S. Navy pilot; who could carve out a new career in the Texas oil patch after being reared in one of Connecticut's upscale families; and who could turn political reversals into renewals on his path to the White House. Most of all he demonstrated that when a person reached 80, he still retained his identity, one not shared by most 80-year-olds. But not because they were 80. It was because most of them would not have leaped from a plane when they were 55 — or even 25.

There is no older person's mould into which people have to be poured, despite efforts by younger people to attempt it. Betty Friedan felt those efforts when she started dancing in her 50s, and noticed how younger people would smile in condescending bemusement that some-one her age would not content herself with sitting in a corner as one of the "oldies." They could see she was dancing. What they could not see was its being as natural for her as it was for them.

That should not surprise us though. A function of myth is to give cohesion to a society — or in this case, a segment of it. When people all understand their world in the same mythical way, they have a tighter bonding with one another. So younger people can feel more identity with each other when they force a different one on older people. But in a time when television audiences crave "reality," is this for real? Especially, is it something older people must accept?

Some don't. Like Walter Zwig, a Canadian developer now in his 80s, who refuses to let the world of business pass him by. He still spends nine months of the year in Toronto, where he has built six million square feet of office space in 13 towers, and now functions as a consultant and corporate board member. If his is an example that not every octogenarian can follow, that makes the point. Older people are not all alike because they were not alike when they were young either.

Especially when they know the uniformity of age is a myth — just like the next familiar distortion.

"THEY CAN'T LEARN ANYTHING NEW"

If that were fact instead of myth, the personal computer industry would not have taken the quantum leaps of expansion that it did in the last two decades of the 20th century. Not all the PCs of the world were bought by people under 60. Still less under 30. Personal Computer sales soared into space partly because so many older people found they could use them as readily as their children and grandchildren could. The essential attribute was not to be young but to be ready to learn.

But isn't it harder to learn when you're older? If they will admit it, people who resist having to learn anything new in their older years probably found learning a challenge when they were young.

When the Canadian government started to restrict the Newfoundland cod fishing industry because the Grand Banks were being "fished out," programs were announced to provide "retraining" of fishers in lines of work that had a better future. But many scorned the offers. One man spoke for others when he shouted at a TV reporter: "Retraining! They gotta be kidding. What can ya learn at 57?" He assumed that his rhetorical question should torpedo the government proposal. But his question could have had an answer. It would have been: "Quite a lot."

For five years, I held a mutual fund dealer's license for which I had to qualify by writing an examination at age 70 in a hall filled with aspiring financial planners in their 20s. My experience was not unique. Not even unusual. University courses of all kinds are including people wanting to launch out into the deep of a second or even third career when they are 57. Or older.

In my last year as a teaching professor, two of my students were aged 60. Both were newly retired school principals. Both achieved high standing in their examinations. Both went on to impressive achievements in their second careers when they were 63.

The myth that older people cannot or will not learn new facts and skills is an outdated buttress misused to hold up age discrimination by employers against older people looking for work.

Those enlightened enough to treat applicants equally and hire people on their merits have demonstrated how readily older people can be integrated into a work force that demands they learn different techniques.

In Britain, B and Q — a chain of do-it-yourself stores — opened one store that was totally staffed by older workers. Was it a disaster because the staff could not keep up with the public? The results were a rebuttal of everything this time-worn myth had persuaded people to believe about older workers. This store had six times less employee turnover than the other stores in the chain, 40% less absenteeism, and — underline this — 18 times the profitability.

Human resources experience has also shown that where older people have difficulty learning new methods, the problem lies not simply in mental or physical limitations. It lies more in the attitudes both teacher and student bring to the task. Learning increases as a challenge if everyone assumes it is more difficult for someone past a prejudged age. Once the myth is dispelled, however, learning can surge forward.

Like the legendary Greek hero Ulysses exhorting his old comrades to launch out on one more voyage to seek the lost continent of Atlantis, older people can now say to one another as they welcome new technology and new knowledge: "Come my friends, 'tis not too late to seek a newer world."

But seeking it demands that we first dispel another myth, one that is more powerful still because it contains just enough truth to convince people.

"THEY CAN'T REMEMBER ANYTHING"

Memory loss can be due to changes in the brain, such as atrophy of the cerebral cortex, plus an accrual of fibrous whorls and tangles in the nerve cells, as well as the accumulation of a kind of plaque. When that happens, the brain will not function as it should, with memory loss being part of the dysfunction. Because this debilitation occurs among older people more than younger, many assume it is part of aging. But it does not have to be.

In *Aging with Grace,* Dr. David Snowdon describes a unique research study among members of the School Sisters of Notre Dame to seek the cause of Alzheimer's disease. An extended period of study did not lead the researchers to the cause, but it did lead them to some conclusions, one of them being that "Alzheimer's is not an inevitable consequence of aging."

Yes, memory loss and other deficiencies are found more often among older people, but not among all older people. Only three percent of people between 65 and 74 show symptoms of Alzheimer's disease. Nor are these deficiencies found exclusively among older people, as Alzheimer's can strike younger people as well.

In 35 years of university teaching, I was impressed by the fact that young people forget too, especially on examinations — and often for the same reason that older people forget. Some of us just let our "memory muscles" atrophy through lack of exercise.

Whatever our age, we do better when we work at remembering. Like the pastor of a thriving Montreal inner city church who spends 30 minutes a day memorizing verses of the Bible so that he can have them available for instant recall when he needs them. The message is that he is doing with his memory what so many people do with their bodies. He is giving it daily exercise to keep it fit. And people can do it at an advanced age too.

Cato the Elder (234–149 B.C.) opposed the influence of Greek culture among his fellow Romans, but with the wisdom of the adage, "Know your enemy," he started to learn the Greek language at 80! When asked why — at his age — he was going through the agony of memorizing grammar and vocabulary, he reminded his inquisitors: "Well, I can't start it any younger." But that was not all. Cato was free from the myth that to be older is to be forgetful and that older people cannot learn anything new.

Phrases such as "senior's moment" subtly bind us to this myth. They express ageism more than reality because older people — like younger people — can modify memory loss when they train their memories to function well. This is not obvious to us in a culture that reduces the importance of memory by making so much technologically available information always on hand. It is more appreciated in those cultures that put their educational emphasis on memorizing long passages of sacred scriptures and literary classics. Those cultures may be deficient in equipping youths to take their place in the "Information Age," but they do offer one advantage — the development of acute memories. Is it too much for older people to work at it too? In remembering names, for example?

One reason Franklin D. Roosevelt (1882–1945) enjoyed such sweeping victories in the 1932 and 1936 presidential elections was the political network his campaign manager, Jim Farley (1888–1973), had built over the years. FDR said this big and genial Irishman knew 10,000 people by name! But Farley himself said the number was closer to 50,000. He demonstrated it by not only calling by name people he might not have seen for years, but mentioning something about their family or town or business, something that showed the person he was important in Jim Farley's eyes, important enough to be recognized.

Developing that mammoth memory bank required Farley to work methodically at remembering the name of everyone he met. The method included his repeating the name several times during the conversation, then writing it down, then filing it, and from time to time going through his file to recall names and join them to faces and renew the circumstances under which he had met the person.

Farley, however, was not the first to appreciate how important remembering names could be. One of Napoleon Bonaparte's nephews advanced from the shadows of Parisian society to become Napoleon III, Emperor of France, partly because he worked assiduously at remembering the name of anyone he met. He worked so hard at it that he claimed he could recall the name of anyone he had ever known, especially if he thought a person he was just meeting might some day be use-

ful to him. He always wrote their name down and consciously committed it to memory so that some day at the right moment, he could call
that name up.

Although Lyndon B. Johnson left the Oval Office as the U.S. president blamed for escalating the Vietnam War, he should be remembered
for a host of social programs that at least addressed the way America was
becoming a country of unacceptable inequities, especially in securing
civil rights for African-Americans.

Among the reasons LBJ was more effective than many presidents at
gaining his way was his having used his long congressional years to build
a network of officials — some of them well down the bureaucracy —
whom he had met as a congressman or senator and could still call by
name when he would telephone them for information. What an impact
it must have been for a civil servant to answer the phone and hear the
president's voice at the other end calling him or her by name. But it
was possible because the president had kept exercising his memory and
could still use it when he was past what many people assume should be
the retirement age.

Memory, like any faculty, needs to be exercised. None of us needs to
assume that because we reach a certain age, we have to become forgetful. It's a myth. Like the next one.

"THEY DON'T FIT IN EASILY"

True, some older people don't. Just as some younger people don't. But
not because they are older or younger. It is more a matter of individual psychology.

Some older people are "loners" because they have always been that
way. Some men and women are always "agin the government" when
they are older because they were gripers when they were younger.
Submitting to rules gladly and fitting into arrangements willingly has
never been their style. But it has little to do with age. People who
worked with others easily in their youth can usually do it just as well
later on. Adaptability is a trait which varies among us as people inde-
pendently of age.

Older people, of course, have had a longer time in which to get used
to one way of doing things, and can understandably feel more reluctant

to let the old order go. But the great social changes of the 20th century were often initiated and supported by older people.

John XXIII (1881–1963) must go down in papal history for his convening the Second Vatican Council which made so many changes in the worship of the world's billion Roman Catholics, the governance of their church, and the scholarly scope of their theologians. But he was 77 when he was elected pope, an age when he could have been expected to cling to things as they were, to insist that "as it was in the beginning, is now and ever shall be." Yet at that age he threw open the windows of the Vatican to let winds of change blow in. His age notwithstanding, this pope saw how his Church needed updating if it was to fit the world of its time. But it was not easy for all his people to see it.

When the new rules for Sunday worship were promulgated, each bishop had to call a clergy conference to explain the "new order." After one bishop finished his address, one of his older pastors asked: "Bishop, I'm nearly 70. At my age, couldn't I finish up with the old Mass I've said since I was ordained?" But the bishop put him straight with an admonition that could apply to any older (or younger) person in any walk of life: "If John XXIII was not too old to change, neither are you!"

Creative as the pope was, he was not a unique example of thinking new thoughts when one is older. In his engaging reflection, *The Virtues of Aging*, former president Jimmy Carter (b. 1924) reminds us of how many people are contributing to the world despite their being in their eighth or even ninth decades. Esther Peterson was Carter's assistant for consumer affairs when she was in her 70s, but when compared to others he cites, she was just getting started. Admiral Hyman Rickover remained in charge of the nuclear submarine program until former president Reagan forced him to retire at age 82 — not much older than Reagan himself. When he was 84, Norman Borland was still active as an agricultural scientist in Ghana, Ethiopia, Mali, Mozambique and Burkina Faso. At age 86, Rioiche Sasakawa financed a program to teach African farmers how to increase their food production.

People that found their security in the familiar when they were younger often find it there when they grow older. But at neither age nor stage does that depend on their years. It is a matter of psychological need. Older people can learn new methods as long as they open their minds to them, are given clear instructions and a supportive work environment.

Recognizing that is why some employers are at last looking for older workers. They have discarded this kind of age prejudice with its stereotype of men and women being unable to fit in with a new organization, new bosses, new coworkers, new everything right at the time when — so the myth goes — people have to follow the same routine or become disoriented.

In one of my favorite McDonald's restaurants, I'm always impressed at how the staff rebuts that prejudice. Older women fill orders and make change alongside teenage students eagerly holding down their first jobs. The women could be grandmothers of the students, but this does not seem to bother either of them. They just get on with the work, and one senses they are just getting on with life that way too. It's a picture of what society should be — and can be when we prefer reality to mythology.

And that is true of more than the workplace.

"THEY'RE ALL DE-SEXED"

It is seldom easy for sons and daughters to accept how they came into the world, since each generation seems to assume they were born after an immaculate conception. But if children find it challenging to acknowledge the sex life of their parents, they find it even more difficult to accept their grandparents — or anyone of their generation — still having sex. It can seem almost obscene.

There is a kernel of truth in the myth that older people have been "neutered," but only a kernel. In many men, though not all, the sex drive dissipates with age, and the loss is often accelerated by prostate surgery or other physical conditions. But neither change should be assumed for every older man.

The pioneering *Kinsey Report on the Sexual Behavior of the American Man,* as far back as 1953, informed us that 70% of men aged 68 were still sexually active. Many question the validity of Kinsey's statistics now, but no one challenges the point this pioneer of scientific sexology was making. Not long after Kinsey did his work, for example, 6,000 persons in *Who's Who* were surveyed, and of the 800 who were 65 years or over who replied, 70% of the married men were still enjoying a regular sex life, and of 104 men between ages 75 and 93, half claimed to be having normal ejaculations. Six of them had sex over eight times a month. So the myth that older men are de-sexed does not hold up when the facts are sought. And the myth has been taking an even stronger beating recently.

Now that pharmaceuticals promise to overcome "erectile dysfunction" among men who find it physically impossible to copulate, the myth that older men cannot have a love life may soon be as impotent as older men have so long been thought to be.

Viagra was the pioneer of this new potential for older men, but it is being joined by others. Nor should it cause people to wonder when they find older women turning to cosmetic surgery, fashionable clothing, beauty care, healthy nutrition, and regular exercise as ways of showing they can still attract men. Why shouldn't they look as romantic outside as their hearts are inside? Though age can wither it, surgery can make a face look new, and justify someone inserting this kind of advertisement in a Saturday newspaper:

"A very loving, petite, fit, cute, 61 year old woman . . . is looking for a caring, romantic man."

In the 20th century, the Pill revolutionized sex for younger people by liberating them from the danger of pregnancy. In the 21st century, pharmaceuticals can make the same radical change in the sex lives of older people. Both men and women can go on feeling fully human, and not a bit like the next myth that insists older people must be different from everyone else.

"THEY'RE OUT OF DATE"

Some older people are. But only because they want to be. Not because they're older. The Information Age is for older people as much as younger people, there now being almost no reason why an older man or woman cannot stay as informed as anyone else.

Large-type books, the Internet, CDs, and videos are on hand to help people of any age inform themselves on any subject. Community groups include opportunities for people of all ages to discuss current books, the latest financial news, and anything else that concerns men and woman who want to stay up-to-date. Older people who are out-

of-date want to be. They do not have to be because they are over 60.
Or over 80.

Some people justly claim they cannot read as well as they had because
of failing eyesight. This is true, but it is not a simple problem of aging.
Some older people retain acute eyesight. Others are able to read easily
once they have surgery. On its own, age does not condemn people to
live with only the knowledge they gained in youth — unless they content
themselves with it.

Was Albert Einstein (1879–1955) out of date at age 63 when he wrote
to then-president Roosevelt advising him that an atomic bomb was feasible in 1942? His letter, which contributed to Roosevelt expediting
the Manhattan Project, was instrumental in starting the age of nuclear
energy — possibly the biggest development of a century of big developments. That does not sound like a person being out of date at 63.

At the other end of life, Einstein had been just as creative in his
younger days. He achieved world fame when, at 26 years old, he
espoused his first theory of relativity and only four years later became a
full professor at the University of Zurich. Age was irrelevant to his
being ahead of the world when he was in his 20s or in his 60s. In his
last decade, he worked assiduously on his "Field Theory," persevering
in his quest for a final answer to the question, "How did the world
begin?" He might have been old but he was not out of date. Einstein
was ahead of his time.

Few people can be that, but most of us can keep up with the times. We
do not have to be Einsteins to make learning a life-long adventure.
Most of us can learn something every day if we are ready to make even
a minimal effort. The subject matter does not have to be esoteric or
sophisticated. Whatever be their interests, being out-of-date is a mistake older people can avoid unless they are determined to bury themselves intellectually.

It may be uncomfortable for some older people to acquire new
knowledge or even to have it given to them effortlessly. They feel cozy
just with what they know. But that is not a necessary or universal characteristic of older people at all. It does not have to go with aging unless
men and women choose to equate the march of time with the retreat
of knowledge.

An organization like Elder hostel demonstrates how hungry for new knowledge older people can be. Its tours and seminars open the information door to men and women hungry to learn new facts, see new sights, find new understanding. Languages, cultures, religions, and histories are on the programs Elderhostel offers for people who want to fill their older years with new knowledge. But some people look for more adventurous learning.

Forced to retire at age 65 from the University of Victoria faculty, R. Vance Peavy (1929–2002) launched a new career for himself in what he called "Socio-Dynamic Counseling," based on the question he put to his clients, "How should I fashion my life?" If this British Columbia academic could not teach in a university classroom, he could learn how to develop and share a new subject with others. But updating is not only a matter of gaining intellectual knowledge. Older people can explode another myth about aging.

"THEY CAN'T KEEP UP"

Older people can update their physical skills so much that they can engage in competitive sports, some for the first time in their lives. In the 1999 Seniors' Games, with participants from all 50 states, 25% of the athletes were in their 50s, 43% in their 60s, 26% in their 70s, and 0.4% in their 90s. But none of them were good enough for those games by accident, or because they had been good in their youth. Regular workouts, learning from coaches, and studying the masters were all in the mix of what made them ready for national competition.

All of this challenges the uncritically accepted — but not factually based — myth that older people tire easily, lack strength, have limited energy, and that they are incapable of doing anything like a decent day's work. This is true only in relative terms. A young runner can usually outpace an older runner, but not always. Not every young runner can go faster than every older runner. It depends on individual ability, acquired knowledge, committed purpose, even personal encouragement. None of them has the slightest dependency on age. Physical results depend on other factors that are open to older people — such a healthy diet, regular exercise, and positive thinking.

Ed Whitlock lives in Milton, Ontario, once a small country town that has now become one of the many commuter communities that make the Greater Toronto Area one of North America's major urban centers. But Milton is not all that has changed. Ed has changed the age myth. He has trounced it, trashed it, and tossed it. How? By running faster than anyone his age — 72 years — and becoming the first person of that age to run the marathon in under three hours. Yet great as that was, his achievement was not the only feat that put *finished* to this age myth.

Fauja Singh, at age 92, became the first runner of the 90-plus class in the world to run the marathon in under six hours. He finished this superman run in five hours, 40 minutes and four seconds.

We are told people go into physical decline after age 25, but the speed and extent of the decline can vary with the lifestyle of the individual. Someone in his 70s can beat someone in his 40s at squash if the winner has been living a healthy life and the loser has over-eaten, over-drunk, and over-smoked.

Jesse Hyde proved this when he walked across the finish line of a 75-mile, 24-hour hike to celebrate his 75th birthday in 1966. Jesse had started hiking in 1913 and since then, had logged 70,000 miles, including several 500-mile treks, a thousand-mile trek, and — on his 69th birthday — a 28-mile marathon run. But that was only one way Hyde's life helped to explode the aging myth.

When he retired from the insurance company where he had worked for 35 years, Hyde devoted his energy to helping other people by mowing 21 lawns a week.

Why labor this point? Because more and more people are refusing to let the calendar dictate their lives. They are also rejecting the myth about aging as a one-way ticket to inertia. More are becoming like Oliver Mefford, who found at age 92 that he must surrender his pilot's license. Rather than thinking that meant "couch potato" was the only future left for him, Mefford discovered an activity which did not require a license and therefore had no legal age restrictions. He could do it at 92 as legally as at 32. So he took it up . . . sky diving!

Mefford may be unusual in his choice of sky diving, but not in his being active. Gerontologist Bernice Neugarten says "half of everyone from 75 to 84 are free of health problems that require special care or for them to curb their activities."

In the 20th century, gerontology — the systematic study of aging as it is and not as mythology has misrepresented it — began to prepare the way for the coming age revolution. This was vital because history shows that an essential preliminary condition to every great revolution comes with the intellectuals transferring their commitment from the *ancien régime* to the new order, from traditional concepts to creative ones.

In 1980, Robert C. Atchley gave us an example of this in *The Social Forces in Later Life* where he listed 23 accurate beliefs about older people that defied 20th-century assumptions. Instead of leading the laid back, scaled-down lives society was assuming the elders had to endure, Atchley asserted the opposite was reality. True, often aging brought limitations a person did not know before, but they were not the whole of an older person's life.

In short, older people are very much like younger people — except for being older.

"THEY . . . "

All ageist myths make a common impact. It is the dehumanization of older people. How? By forcing men and women into an undifferentiated lump that denies them the individuality without which none of us is fully human. A familiar phrase like "They say . . ." shows this because we do not know who the "they" are. Instead we speak about a faceless, nameless somebody we call "they," and this dehumanized language points to dehumanized relationships and then dehumanized persons.

In *The Encyclopedia of Aging*, ageism is defined as a "process of systematic stereotyping of and discrimination against people because they are old."

We can discriminate against anyone if we think of him or her chiefly in terms of a category — be it religious, racial, ethnic, income, anything — instead of respecting him or her as someone with a name, an individual like ourselves.

Commanding respect is not easy when the culture encourages both young and old to think of age in these mythological ways. Electronic media does this by presenting older people in a patronizing way as largely dependent, often confused, sometimes comical persons. The media once did that with women and racial minorities, and a priority change enforced by the age revolution will be giving this media distortion of older people an overdue funeral in the 21st century.

It will not be easy because discrimination against older people has been so available. They are so physically obvious and can be readily picked out in any crowd. But that was just as true of women and racial minorities before the gender and race revolutions put an end to the discrimination they had had to suffer silently for so long. The age revolution will be just as effective in ridding the culture of its ageist humor, derision, and condescension. It will succeed in its demand that older people be seen as persons who have lost none of their humanity by losing some of their youthful energy. And it will begin by dealing with age mythology.

When we treat one others as less than persons, we rob them of something precious to their being fully human. And that's the fallacy in these myths. Each one implies an older person is not "he" or "she" but just part of a "they."

All the generic terms which have evolved over time reinforce this mythological distortion because they perceive older men and women as no more than members of a category. It can be labeled "Senior Citizen," a term used so widely that most people fail to see how dehumanizing it is with its label-like utility function of telling us what the person — like a thing — is. It shapes the image of what being older means in the minds of younger people. Worse, it shapes the image in the minds of older people themselves. And reinforces, in both minds, thinking of an older person as part of the "they."

That is why the age revolution will involve demythologization. It will include not only ridding ourselves of the myths on their own, but also recognizing what these myths tell us about our culture. They tell us that aging — when perceived in these mythological terms — means accepting oneself as a lesser breed, as part of a chronological cohort that is easing itself down the hill.

So the coming age revolution begins with ridding ourselves of that concept, and that starts with dispelling the myths that press it down deep into the psyches of older people. Once they are free, older people can think revolutionary thoughts about themselves and their place in the world. It can begin with thinking they still have a place in the world of work.

In summary, relationships between older and younger people can be twisted by myths about aging that do not respect how elders demonstrate that they, like their younger contemporaries, show individual differences.

These myths include such common generalizations as elders are "all alike," "can't learn anything new," "can't remember anything," "don't fit in," "are de-sexed," and "can't keep up."

CHAPTER 3

Elders at Work

Statistics are usually dull reading, but not always. Sometimes they can be dramatic, like these that foretell a turnaround in the job market.

In 1900, two out of every three American men 65 years of age and over had jobs. Since then, a change in lifestyle has made that seem ancient history. When the 20th century finished, only about one out of every ten of the male population in the United States 65 years of age and up was working for pay outside the home. Retirement had become so commonplace it seemed part of the nature of things.

To speak of an older person going to work referred to someone who could be pitied — or maybe thought a little odd. It seemed unjust, like the denial of a human right, or an eccentricity — something that defied rational explanation. People favored not only retirement at 65, but even earlier. "Freedom 55" became the prize for the harassed middle-aged, commuter-traveling, long-hours-working man or woman.

But should we assume that will last long into the 21st century? Not only are macro-economic changes signaling that revolutionary changes are waiting for older people, a different trail is already being blazed.

According to a Statistics Canada survey, the current trend among people 65 and over is not total retirement but work — maybe part-time, maybe even seasonal, but still work. Out of a total population of 31 million, over 300,000 men and women aged 65-plus were employed in 2001 — almost 20% more than five years earlier. And they were employed at real jobs.

The most popular occupation was farming, followed by retail sales. Among professionals, work drew chiefly from accountants, lawyers, doctors and clergy. And they were not all just a bit over 65. Six percent were in their 80s. Longtime premier of Alberta Peter Lougheed carries a full load at 75 — partnership in a Calgary law firm, membership on seven corporate boards, plus several community service boards. Is it a chore? "I can't even imagine retiring," he says. But he is not really as unusual now as he might have seemed a few years ago.

The coming age revolution means the late Harold Fisher will not seem as unique as he once might have. During his long and productive life, this respected Detroit architect represented the future. Not because he went each business day to his office in Harold H. Fisher and Associates, the firm he founded in 1945, but because he was over 100 years of age!

The oldest known worker in the United States and winner of the National Prime Time Award as "the outstanding older worker of the United States," Fisher felt anything but cheated of some birthright because he was still going to work. He hoped to keep working until he was 110.

As he quipped, "no one can fire you if you own the company." But that was not the only reason. His body, he said, was "as hard as a rock" because of the exercise and weight lifting program he began when he was younger — at a mere 70 years of age. More important, he told people his work was his love, so much so that he stayed with it from his start at age 15 as an apprentice architect. He built his firm up from its 1945 foundation to be one of the leading American centers of church design.

Not only did he love the work enough to go to the office each day dressed for business in suit, shirt and tie, he did more than look the part. He took an active interest in the creative design work that had given the firm its reputation — and its clientele.

But how much significance is there in this kind of centenarian superman? Most people do not even make 100 years of age (although there are 55,000 centenarians in the United States — enough to populate a whole city), and still fewer are able to work at 100 or at any age close to it, so what's the point?

The point is that all our assumptions about aging are open to challenge. Nothing should be taken for granted when we learn of a man like Harold Fisher — or a woman like the late Rose Blumkin, who was still running Mrs. B's Warehouse in Omaha, Nebraska, at age 100 and kept it operating until her death a few years ago.

A local legend long before her centennial, Blumkin's 100th birthday was attended by the governor of the state, a United States senator, a congressman, and the mayor of her city.

Born in Russia, Blumkin arrived in the United States in 1917 at age 25. Never having attended school in her life, she plunged into work and marriage, and by 1937 she opened the Nebraska Furniture Mart with a capital of $500. Only four feet, ten inches tall, Blumkin soon became a giant in the business community, the store growing and growing because of her policy: "Sell cheap and tell the truth." The store eventually covered 200,000 square feet, supported by a 360,000-square-foot warehouse and surrounded by 10 acres of land. Her company expanded to a flooring business in Lincoln, Nebraska, and a commercial sales office in Des Moines, Iowa.

It was a big load for an aging woman to carry, and in 1983, she mistakenly thought she had had enough. So she sold out to Warren Buffett, almost a neighbor, for $60 million. He paid cash but did not get a non-competition agreement. What was the point when the vendor was past retirement? Well, the impossible happened.

When Blumkin found she could not stand retirement, she opened a new shop, Mrs. B's Warehouse, explaining the move this way: "I live alone now. So that's why I work. I hate to go home. I work to avoid the grave." And she succeeded more than most people: She was working still when she was in her 10th decade, using a battery-operated scooter to get around her huge store.

But dramatic as these examples of Harold Fisher and Rose Blumkin are, how much do they apply to most people? Two human "Mount Everests" do not a mountain range make. In fact, they can make the rest of us look all the smaller — but only if we are determined to feel that way about ourselves. Working when one is older is for "just plain folks" too.

If you go to LAX, as that transportation colossus — the Los Angeles Airport — is called, passengers with walking difficulties may find themselves assisted by a courteous, genial attendant in blue blazer and gray pants who will push them in a wheelchair from the plane to the baggage carousel. Now in his upper 70s, he has been doing his job since he turned 65. And doing it well five days a week, nine to five.

Does he speak of this with remorse? Would he rather be in a seniors' center playing cards? Does he feel cheated by Social Security's not paying him enough to join the leisure class? Although his hair is silver, his smile is bright and his voice strong when he speaks of his work. He does not head a firm or own a store like Fisher or Blumkin, but he is just as conscious of his rendering a service to the needs of his fellow humans. And he is not alone.

Step into a Wal-Mart store and you are likely to be given a warm welcome by an older man or woman with a bright smile and a stretched out hand. Is this hokey? A cornball gimmick you might expect from a company that started in Arkansas? Not many people are indifferent to a friendly greeting, especially when they are accustomed to the cold impersonality of today's big box store culture. Wal-Mart is on to something in hiring older people to be their greeters, and so are other "big cap" service providers.

McDonald's has been doing it for years, gray heads working alongside rosy cheeks behind the counters of the world's largest restaurant chain. Day's Inn has learned older people make excellent reservation agents. Travelers Insurance claims it saves a million dollars a year in employment agency commissions by running its own job bank of retired employees who are ready to come in on a "when needed" basis. Radio Shack is another company that has discovered older employees have something special to offer. Like wanting to help customers find exactly what they need.

Harold Fisher and Rose Blumkin are not unique. Just superlative examples of how the future is already with us. The coming age revolution will return older men and women to the workplace. The trend has already begun.

Riding this wave of the future is someone like Robert Salter who, after a lifetime of working seven days a week, cut it down to five when he turned 70 years old.

One of the world's leading orthopedic surgeons, Dr. Salter taught surgery at the University of Toronto and practiced it brilliantly enough to attract advanced students from every continent, give lectures at over 50 universities, and become a Companion of the Order of Canada, his country's highest honor. But as he nears 80, he is still donning his white lab coat each day, Monday through Friday, and researching new and better surgical techniques.

Through his research, surgical knowledge is advanced even though Dr. Salter has every right to spend his days loafing after a lifetime of relentless dedication to science.

Why doesn't he loaf then? If he were that kind of person, he would not have become a world class surgeon in the first place.

Dr. Salter is an example of how older men and women can — and do — have something to offer humanity. Why should he have to stop being productive because he has reached a foreordained age? Instead of the "Freedom 55" advertised by cruise lines and retirement ghettos, he has chosen "Achievement 75" — and may go on to "Still More Achievement 85."

Peter Patterson learned what the words "Golden Parachute" could mean when the insurance company of which he was president and CEO was taken over by another corporation and he was out of a job. Not that he was out of pocket, because his settlement was enough that Peter no longer needed to work for a living. So for several months he did the obvious and enjoyed his newfound leisure to the full. But eventually he found there had to be something more in his life.

It was identity. He did not enjoy being identified only by the job he had once had or by the absence of anything like that in the present. Pleasant as a summer of boating and swimming had been, it was not enough. There was an inner emptiness he felt and did not like. Couldn't he do more with his life than he was doing?

A chance to do more came when he heard about a job made for a person with his experience and knowledge. A college's bursar was retiring and Peter was an obviously perfect fit for the vacant position. With the title of business director, he would take charge of all college activities outside the academic ones. Everyone on staff, apart from the faculty, would report to him. And from the college's standpoint, his arrival brought another benefit. He insisted on working without remuneration because of the settlement agreement he had made with his previous company. Peter also thought he could do the job in only three days a week so that he could devote the other two business days to being chair of a Third World aid non-government organization.

So here we have examples of older people preferring to work than to retire. Some are unbelievably old, some at least a generation younger, yet all still above the early retirement age the late 20th century favored. What they show is that elder employment will be as much part of the 21st century scene as female employment became in the 20th. The trend has already started; as more than 16 million American jobs are held by people 55 years of age or more, and not just among those holding on until they become pensionable — the number of older people getting new jobs is greater than the number of young people taking them. By 2015, the number of employees over 55 will be almost 32 million, far more than the 18.4 million there were in 2000. The unthinkable is taking place before our eyes, and it is going to become the commonplace. Why? Three reasons.

PENSIONS WILL NOT BE ENOUGH

A major drive behind the return of older people to the work force will be the uncertainty of pensions fully funding men and women for the ever extending length of time people are living in retirement. As well, the number of pensioners is growing faster than the number of workers contributing to pension funds. To make the problem a potential crisis, economic growth that is essential to the financial capability of pension funds cannot be taken for granted any longer. In 2003, it was estimated that it could cost employers 1.5 trillion U.S. dollars to make up the shortfall in pension funds.

Can it be done? The time is near when all the late-20th-century assumptions of enjoying a permanent, fully funded vacation at a fixed age can lack reality. It is a serious threat. Despite the impressive entitlement programs so many western countries provide, poverty remains more common among the elderly than the young. It could become worse if the age revolution did not re-open earning doors to older people. This is especially vital to people wanting to retire early. There should be enough for people that do not start to draw pensions until age 65, but dreams of going early and being paid forever are now in doubt. How has this threatened reversal happened?

When Social Security was initiated in 1935, nine Americans were working and paying into the fund for every pensioner who would draw the first payments. But compare that with the radical change that occurred as the United States neared the 21st century. By 1990, instead of nine workers contributing to Social Security for every pensioner receiving benefits, only 3.3 were. But that is the not the end of the threat. By 2010, there will be only two workers contributing for each pensioner drawing. Even though Congress has already increased the age of eligibility to avert a crisis, the change will not take full effect until 2027. Will this measure be enough?

Older Americans are living longer (again, the United States has 55,000 people aged 100 or more) and this elder population is escalating faster than any other age sector (centenarians have tripled in number since 1980). The trend will not stop or even slow down. In the year 2000, there were 35 million men and women aged 65 years and over — more than the entire population during the Civil War, and more than enough to populate Canada now. If that seems critical to pension planning, think what it means to project — as demographic experts do — an elder growth to 64.5 million by 2030. That's only one generation away, and a total larger than the populations of most of the world's countries.

To compound this financial threat, the late 20th century saw a myopic enthusiasm inspire an "early retirement bubble." It produced results that brought short-term gain, but now threaten long-term pain. In 1970, half of American men were still employed at age 65, but by 1993, only 30% were. In the 1960s, early retirement benefits were claimed by only 18% of American men, but by 2000, a dangerous 73% of retirees were claiming their pensions early. Where at the start of the century, three out of every four older men were working for pay, only one out of every five was at the century's end. But this threat is standing over not only the United States. It has made Canada home to the only 100% income tax in the democratic world.

In 1953, Canada introduced a universal old age security pension based solely on age and not on need. For a full generation, it seemed fiscally plausible, but by the last decade of the century, it no longer was.

So the government introduced the OAS Recovery Tax — popularly renamed the "clawback" — which requires older people whose income exceeds a determined figure to pay back a percentage of the pension.

This "clawback" is graduated according to income so that a more affluent pensioner pays the entire Old Age Security Pension back. In fact, he or she no longer pays it back because when a taxable income reaches a stated figure, the pension is not even received. This so-called taxation is really confiscation. But extreme as 100% taxation is, it may not be enough as a single solution to a national problem.

By 2016, Canada will have more people leaving the work force than entering it. The pension plans that seemed so plausible at mid century are losing their long-term viability. As one example we can look at the Anglican Church of Canada's pension plan, which in three short years, 1999 to 2002, went from having more contributors than pensioners to just the opposite. As a result, the fund was not able to support an increase in accrued pension for the first time in 40 years. The plan's investments had enjoyed a 15% return in 2003, but that was not enough to balance the fund having more people taking out than paying in. Maybe that was only a straw in the wind. But wasn't it enough to tell us how the wind is starting to blow?

Throughout the western world, this crisis is threatening every country that embraced the now outmoded assumptions about aging. Too many people are leaving the work force and too few are entering it. Life-extending pharmaceuticals at one end and birth-preventing pharmaceuticals at the other create the makings of a crisis. It can be averted by an age revolution that tells us people do not have to retire fully at the age the 20th century assumed work should end. Economic disaster can be averted best when the age revolution convinces people that we do not have to leave income-generating work at a fixed age and live as though we were on a permanent vacation. The term "idle rich" is viable only as long as there are just a few people living that way. When the majority wants to do it at 65 — or earlier — there's going to be trouble. Big time. Especially when a hoped-for solution has too many holes.

Not everyone can avert it by supplementing pensions with personal retirement funds, such as the RRSP in Canada and the IRA in the United States. These are popular for obvious reasons. They give people two direct benefits. One, they provide a way of saving money and deferring taxes at the same time. Second, they ensure the person has a nest egg in the future when the earning years come to an end.

What they do not protect a person against, however, is the financial threat that comes with living a long, long time. The fastest growing sector of the population in both Canada and the United States is the "old old" — those 85 years and over. What can seem an ample money supply at 65 may not be once they are 85 or 90 or more. Especially when a person may have to enter a care community or hire help that will come in. Inflation alone can erode a person's future too. Even if it is stable, it will reduce the purchasing power of a dollar by 20% over 10 years, and unless people have ways of increasing their retirement wealth as they grow older and older, they may find themselves in difficulty just when they are least capable of coping with it.

One solution is delaying the time when a person is living solely on retirement income. Even working part-time — so many days a week or so many months of the year — may add enough to make the difference between financial peace and anxiety.

The North American recession of 2000 and the prolonged "bear market" showed people they should no longer take for granted that the future could be guaranteed. In the late 1990s, when youthful entrepreneurs and financiers could boast of becoming millionaires by 25, the older generation could take seriously their dreams of financing a life of playing golf every day they were not on a cruise. Then people discovered that the business cycle actually had not been abolished, that the law of investment gravity was inexorable. What goes up in the market will some day come down.

According to a 2002 *Business Week*/Harris poll, the investment portfolio of over half the retirees with incomes of $85,000 or more had lost 25% of their market value in the previous two years. Typical was a woman who sold her insurance business in an upstate New York town in 2000 with the then-plausible explanation that the sale would finance her until her Social Security payments would start, and her retirement investment portfolio would add enough to keep her independent. Plausible? Yes, very much so. It just did not work out that way. Like millions of other Americans and Canadians, she was overtaken by events.

Just two years later, that dream future became a nightmare. The payments from her business had stopped. The collapse of the stock market had slashed her portfolio value from over a million to $600,000. Instead of enjoying restaurant meals and foreign travel as a lifestyle, she had to start looking at ads for part-time jobs and to recognize that she might even need to work full-time just to keep going. It was painful for a person who had every right to think she had provided for her older years. But her experience showed the direction the future was taking, and earning an income as long as one can will become the 21st century rule of thumb.

If people at 65 could be sure they'd be gone by 75, they could blow their bundle in 10 years of high living. But since they may reach 85 or live longer, they have to stretch it out. Retirement can still remain possible, but it may be partial rather than total at the start. The trend has already begun.

In the mid-1980s only 16% of Americans aged 65 or over were still earning — down from 36% in 1962. But by the late 1990s, the curve was swinging up with 21% of older Americans earning income.

Part of this trend is the growing number of older people who create their own jobs, self-employment enjoying a revival after decades of abeyance. Almost one of every three Canadians working at age 55 or more is self-employed. Another dimension of the trend is people working in the expanding service sector when the job does not require heavy responsibility or heavy physical effort.

One way or another, older people who find themselves financially challenged see that the solution lies in earning a partial income instead of beating on the doors of government. That's one reason why 5,000 people visit the Senior Job Bank web site every day. Finding enough work to pay the bills remains the challenge many thought they had put behind them.

Isn't that an outrageous prospect though? No way. The coming age revolution will see people working longer for a second reason.

WORK IS FULFILLING

Some people are stuck with jobs so barren of personal satisfaction that retirement is liberation. Others are doing jobs that demand so much physical effort that the last few years on the job are a struggle — a daily struggle. Then there are men and women who can't wait to get out from under a boss who turns the workplace into a boot camp. Let's face reality. Some people count the days until their pension will let them cheer: "Free at last. Free at last. Thank God almighty, I'm free at last." But not everyone feels that way.

Katherine Graham was one. The need for income was not a priority to this septuagenarian when she recognized it was time to step down from the throne of her publishing empire that included the *Washington Post* and *Newsweek*. Born to wealth, she had never known financial need, and when her husband died, she might have been expected to let others run the business he had headed so ably. What did she know about publishing? Business? Anything?

What she knew was that she wanted to try, and try she did — with brilliant success. But that was in her mid-40s. What about the challenge of her 70s? Graham was happy to return to playing bridge as well as taking up golf, but only on the margin of her life. She had to keep working. As she phrased it in her best selling *Personal History*: "I knew that I essentially never wanted not to work. To me, working is a form of sustenance, like food or water, and as nearly essential."

Working for pay was not a priority for her. Working for fulfillment was. So she turned her efforts to things that could provide the inner sustenance she needed. Helping others get the education they might have been denied was one. To do it, she helped launch an early childhood education project in a Washington neighborhood that aimed at helping parents involve themselves in their children's learning.

In addition, she began writing a book, something she had not done before. It would be about herself, one that would describe her inner struggle and her victory in such a way that others could take courage with their challenges. And write it she did. A 642-page book that became an instant bestseller because it shared with readers the human condition so many of them had felt. But were those "retirement projects" real work?

Since her objective was not income, many people might not put them down as examples of real work because they are convinced nothing is unless you get paid for it. But what was Blessed Mother Theresa

(1910–97) paid for her lifetime of work among the poor of Calcutta? Since she herself was living under a vow of poverty, she could take no income from anything she did, including the operation of a network of service communities on three continents. Did that mean none of it was work? It brought her world recognition, including the Pope John XXIII Peace Prize and the Nobel Peace Prize. But since she was not on salary, did she have a real job?

That question will not be asked once the age revolution liberates our minds from the prejudice that if you do a job as a volunteer, you are not truly part of the labor force. We will respect how many men and women keep on working even though they may terminate working for pay. We will also respect something old that is new again.

Since the Industrial Revolution took people off their farms and out of their cottages to labor in mills and factories, we have assumed people have to "go to work" to be really working. Housewives were thus put down because they worked at home, and for generations that did not rate as real work. A child care worker in a nursery school could be recognized as working, but not a mother looking after her own children at home. Yet the gender revolution of the 20th century changed that misperception. The age revolution of the 21st will change it for older people who work out of their homes.

People like Donald Wheeler who, since retiring as a college professor of business, has worked part-time as an advocate for challenged people. Don's work is not helping them directly with their difficulties, but assisting them to gain access to programs and services they need but may have been denied, such as one child who could be described as having a four-year-old's mind in a 13-year-old's body. When she was denied speech therapy at the age of six, Don persuaded hospital and government authorities to look at her case again. They did and she was admitted to the programs she needed.

An older man, visiting his hospitalized wife each day, was denied access to the hospital cafeteria even though it meant his having to go out in the freezing cold to find a restaurant. Don went to bat for him until common decency prevailed and the man was permitted to buy a meal in the hospital.

If Don were on the payroll of a government agency, his advocacy work would be called his job. But since he does it as a volunteer and works out of his home, he is labeled "retired" and his service to others is viewed as a kind of hobby. This is a condescending put-down by a money-driven culture, but not forever.

Such sentiments will change as the 21st century recognizes society could not function without the uncounted army of volunteers who work for nothing except the personal satisfaction of doing something useful for others. These people do not need incomes, but they do need something they find in work that they cannot find anywhere else.

For far more people than can be numbered, working is not just a living, it's part of life. The freedom to fill their days with fun and games has no appeal. Along with the economic challenges that threaten old-style retirement plans, there is this second reason why older people should be free to work, and it is another reason why the 21st century will bring the end of mandatory retirement in all jurisdictions not enlightened enough to have abolished it in the 20th. The need for this was foreseen by one of the great gurus of American management practices as long ago as 1972.

In *The Unseen Revolution,* Peter Drucker argued that mandatory retirement would end, and at the time his prophecy was scoffed at by all who thought retiring early should be the goal. But only six years later, it was abolished in California. The coming age revolution will confirm Drucker's judgment. In *Towards the Next Economics,* Drucker wrote that mandatory and fixed retirement is both unethical and wasteful: "Mandatory retirement at 65 condemns to idleness and uselessness a great many healthy people who want to work, if only part-time."

Drucker did not advocate people staying in charge of enterprises indefinitely, just that people should have the freedom to go on working in some capacity that they were still able to fill effectively.

The United States has already abolished mandatory retirement regulations in most parts of the country, and so has Canada in the federal public service, with some of the provinces following suit. None of those actions has threatened retirement itself, the object being something else altogether. Retirement is going to stay, but it is not going to stay the same. Retirement as we knew it in the late 20th century will not last long in the 21st. Instead of being mandatory, fixed, and total, its future is to be voluntary, flexible, and partial. Where people just want to work

— whether for income or satisfaction — the age revolution will mean the barriers come down.

In the past, this often was a freedom open only to men or women who were self-employed either in professional practices or in companies they themselves owned. But the doors are starting to open at all levels. When Bill Ford wanted to put his auto company's finances in order in 2002, he did not look for a bright young man full of the latest ideas. Instead he called Allan Gilmour back to become vice-chair and chief financial officer even though Gilmour was 67 and had already retired from the Ford Motor Company in 1995. Yet during those seven years away from Ford, Gilmour had not stopped working. In fact, he had acquired a car dealership. Some people just like to be on the job regardless of what age they are.

Louis Busch is an example of this. He goes to his Malibu, California, real estate office every morning, summer or winter, seven days a week. Busch is out the door of his showplace canyon home early, on his way to the firm he opened shortly after returning from World War II service as a United States Navy pilot. It is in a two-story building he owns with an upstairs apartment where he and his wife, Doris, lived before the business was big enough for them to afford a house for their family of three children.

At the office before anyone else, Louis puts the coffee on and is ready for another day with his staff and his clients, be they people looking for a beach house where they can feast their eyes on the enthralling sunsets over the Pacific, a university wanting to assemble land for a campus, or a business with property looking for a buyer, or maybe just old friends and associates who drop by. He is there all day, every day — at the same stand — still doing business. But why? What keeps him at this Spartan regimen the whole year?

Although he is now 80, Louis takes only a few weeks off each year, one for a cruise with Doris, and one for a cruise with their family, including a son-in-law and a grandson. There must be some reason other than income, since that is clearly not an urgent necessity. In business-like fashion, Louis provides the answer in three short words: "I love it."

That explains everything. He finds the same fulfillment in real estate that the commercials for retirement living tell men and women they can find in leisure. It is not easy for everyone to understand that. But people can enjoy work so much, the demand that they step away from can be more penalty than reward. So why should they have to do it as long as they are capable? The age revolution will mean they won't.

One of the French Revolution's intellectual leaders, the Marquis de Condorcet (1743–94) wrote that the object of a true revolution must be to expand the people's freedoms, and part of the coming age revolution's purpose is to give people freedom of choice where they have been denied it — the workplace.

Jack Dobrow demonstrated there was no good reason for resisting a person's desire to work after passing the usual retirement age. Like the legendary cowboy, he almost died with his boots on by operating Jack's Barber Shop until he was taken to hospital seven weeks before his death at age 83.

It was like the end of an era for neighbors and customers because he had been in business for 52 years in the same location at the heart of Canada's largest city, Toronto. Every time I went into the store he told me proudly that his was one of only three businesses in the city's upscale Deer Park district still open after half a century. He had reason to be proud because sustaining a business for over five decades is never easy, be it a multi-national corporation or a neighborhood store. And Jack had been meeting challenge all his life.

As a young man Jack escaped from Nazi-held Poland in 1939. Then he spent almost six years fighting the Nazis in a Partisan unit. Finally he returned to Poland after World II long enough to marry Polly, an Auschwitz survivor, and with her he made his way to Canada. His new land, he reasoned, was a good place to learn a new trade and he trained as a barber. Within weeks of being licensed, he opened his store and never closed it. Why should he have at 60? 65? 75? 80? Any age?

His barbershop was too big a part of him. It meant not only a living, but also a life. It was a forum for anything that was in the news. Jack was so much its center that some customers dubbed him "the Mayor of St. Clair and Yonge." Retirement could not have given him the fulfillment that work did.

People like Louis Busch and Jack Dobrow show how the age revolution is going to turn a reversal into a renewal. If people find that they will not be able to retire early and live a financially carefree life for decades, that need not alarm them. Louis and Jack show us how people can work even at 80, still make a living, still even run a business and — best of all — still have a full life. And they are not alone.

What would it have meant to Jessica Tandy (1909–94) if she had retired at 65 — or even 79 — instead of continuing to work as one of North America's most respected actors? More time to look at television? More chances to travel? More leisure hours with husband and fellow star, Hume Cronyn? Probably all of the above. But retirement would have also deprived her of something precious.

It would have robbed her of the Oscar she won for her brilliant performance in the motion picture, *Driving Miss Daisy,* which she received when she was 80 years old. And it meant all the more because it was the first time she had been recognized by the Academy of Motion Picture Arts and Sciences despite her decades of five-star performances on stage and screen. Living a long time can mean also achieving a long time. And with that achievement, fulfilling oneself as a person.

The age revolution will open that door of opportunity to people. As Condorcet asserted, a revolution's aim should be to expand people's freedom. This one will do it for older people who want the freedom to be themselves in the workplace.

Research has shown that perhaps a third of the people who retire have trouble adjusting to their new lives. Men and women who had been CEOs found it the most challenging, while others found that not having a job to go to was too much for their spouses as well as themselves. Some rented offices just for that reason. More have sought employment — at the top if that's what they were used to, or right at the bottom if that's what they found easiest to handle.

Some critics protest that seniors still working is another example of "greedy old goats" wanting to hold on to jobs instead of making room for younger people to have their chance. If that was ever a good argument, it is no longer. Just as demographics show all our assumptions about retirement incomes have to be examined all over again, so must our expectations that there will always be a horde of eager youths pounding on the gate of the future.

NOT ENOUGH YOUNG PEOPLE

Just as there may soon be too many old people drawing pensions, so there may not be enough young people wanting to fill retirement vacancies. As the labor force ages and its older members retire, there may be a critical shortage of skilled personnel.

This can remove an economic factor on which the whole retirement structure has rested: the need to displace older people from the work force so that younger people can enter it or move up within it. Since turning older people out was both morally unjust and politically unacceptable, the evolution of retirement on pensions removed the objections to creating job vacancies that could give youth their chance. From Otto von Bismarck's pioneering pension in the late 19th century to Franklin Roosevelt's Social Security system in the 1930s, that was the slow but sure trend in liberal democracies. Later in the 20th century, with the massive youth population spawned by the Baby Boom, that evolution escalated to early retirement dreams catching the imagination of people who had been encouraged to think of retirement as their just reward for a life of labor. But what if the 21st century is beginning with a new reality that threatens this vision? Not only will there not be enough young people to support the ballooning number of retirees, but there will not be enough to replace them. For perhaps the first time in history, older people will not be under pressure to get out of the way.

And massive as that change will be, it can happen.

That's been the message from the dropping fertility rate in most developed countries. This rate is calculated according to the number of children born from the number of adults in their child-bearing years, and it is statistically clear that the rate is nowhere close to what is needed for population growth by natural increase.

Where the American fertility rate had been 3.45 in the years 1960–64, it had dropped to 1.81 just 20 years later. In 1990, there was a resurgence when the fertility rate rose to 2.08 because of the way women 30 years or older were having children after having started their careers. But that fertility upturn did not signal a return to the time when young people could provide a firm base on which the older population could stand.

Women were still having children. But many were having them at an age older than had been the historical norm. And they were having fewer. A fertility rate of 2.1 is said to be the minimum for people to replace themselves, and population growth by natural increase demands a rate higher than that. But that does not seem the probable future at all. Two children per family is closer to it. The later Baby Boomers (people born in the early 1960s) are restricting themselves to small families partly because so many mothers work outside the home, and partly because they start later as parents.

Like other developed countries, Canada has been following the same trend. Where in 1956, almost half the population (46.7%) was under 25 years of age, less than one third was by the end of the century. This trend continuing, it is predicted that only 25% of Canadians will be under 25 by the year 2026.

What is called the rate of potential support (the number of people working per the number of fully retired people) will crash from five-to-one to only three-to-one by 2026. Once there was a crowd of young people standing around any door of opportunity. They were waiting for older people to get out of their way. In the future, there can be so few eager aspirants that a radically new desire to keep some of the "old hands" on will emerge. And that is not the only change.

When so much work in industry demanded youthful strength and energy, older workers were not attractive. But now that the developed world has moved to a service economy with a high use of technology, work by older people is becoming feasible.

But will that be so if there is enough immigration from the Third World — where birth rates remain staggeringly high and where economic deprivation encourages the ambitious to find a way out? Yet this may not be the simple solution it appears to be.

Immigration has often been encouraged chiefly to fill unskilled, low-paid, bottom-end jobs that native-born people have not wanted. It has not been until the second generation that an immigrant family has normally qualified for the skilled jobs.

As well, many immigrants have to meet language and cultural challenges that initially reduce their attraction to employers. So why wouldn't employers rather keep their tried and true staff, especially when they can work out part-time, flex-hours arrangements which are convenient for the worker and cheaper for the employer, no benefits having to be paid?

There's an age revolution coming, and part of it will be the new appeal of older workers an employer can count on at a time when fewer up and coming young people will be available. It will be recognized that among older people, their "get up and go" has not always got up and gone.

In his book, *Why Not the Best?*, President Jimmy Carter recalled the interview he had had as a new graduate of the United States Naval Academy wanting to join the nuclear submarine project which Admiral Hyman Rickover was organizing. A career-life later and after that young ensign had served as president of the United States, this same admiral was still in charge of the nuclear submarine program. In fact he did not retire until he was 82. He need not have stepped down then except for being nudged to do so by Ronald Reagan, himself an octogenarian by that point.

Why should the admiral have left earlier at the age most employers deem the time to give up? None of his scientific work demanded youthful physical strength, and there was no younger person his equal. As long as his mind was clear, his leadership was possible. And he was not unique.

John Kenneth Galbraith (b. 1908) has been advisor to presidents, U.S. ambassador to India, long-time economics professor at Harvard, and writer of pattern-setting books, such as *The Affluent Society,* published at age 93, and *The Economics of Innocent Fraud,* which probes the unethical and often culpable practices taken for granted in the world of investments. In recent years, his physical health has declined enough that, apart from assisted walks in his garden, he was largely confined to his home. But if his body was failing him, there was nothing wrong with his nonagenarian brain when he could produce a work as timely as that.

His work reveals what our stereotyping and mythologizing of age has hidden so long. Galbraith was doing at 93 what he had been doing all his life. His surviving into a 10th decade and continuing to write could be understood when we realize that writing in the face of difficulties was what he had been doing all his career. Somehow he had been not only an economics professor at Harvard University, but involved at the White House, a speech writer for John Kennedy, an intellectual activist within the Democrat party, and a spokesman for his country overseas. All the time he was doing those jobs, he was also writing books. So why would he stop at 93?

Yes, he would have had to if his brain had not stayed clear. But wasn't that just as necessary when he was 63? Or 43? Given the health a worker needs at any age, people can still function when they are old. Even when they are "old old." As eminent as Galbraith is, he is not unique.

Must people have the star quality of a Galbraith to stay on the job? The coming age revolution will give that question a definite "No" as it opens the door to all men and women who like their work enough to keep at it. Social work scholar Lynn McDonald reports that of the men and women who take early retirement, 17% return to work.

Richard Currie retired as CEO of George Weston Ltd., Canada's largest food chain, only to become — at 64 — chair of Bell Canada Enterprises, the country's largest telephone network. He was not unusual. A survey of 656 people aged from 50 to 67 who retired from full-time jobs between 1993 and 1997 showed most of them were back at work, full-or part-time. Some needed income. Others just wanted to work. Their health was good enough, and the kind of work they took did not demand excessive physical effort. Many liked a balance of work and leisure they could not have at the full-time jobs they had left nor in the full-time leisure they had found in retirement. Balance appealed to them more as a lifestyle.

A survey of 586 large American companies claimed that 16 percent had already started to offer "phased retirement" options to their personnel. Another 28% were planning to introduce that alternative within the next two years.

IBM Canada Ltd. had added a retiree-on-call program and reported a roster of 250 men and women willing to come back to work on a "when needed" basis. The Canadian government was also bringing back retired men and women to apply their experience to current demands.

What could have been a crisis in an earlier age need not be even a problem in the 21st century. If there are fewer young people seeking work and if there are more older people needing work to finance themselves, these two unprecedented demographic developments can fit together. It will be part of the coming age revolution. But will it work as easily as all that?

This is my ninth book, six of them written since I turned 65. Through the years, I have published almost 500 articles, columns, and reviews in magazines, newspapers, and journals. Over 100 since I was 65. Unless some younger people can do it better and are eager to replace me, I should carry on just the way Jack Dobrow stayed at his barber's chair and Louis Busch is still selling real estate.

Older people should not expect to hold jobs we cannot do or to keep them when someone else, young or old, can do them better. But if better people are not available, why should older people not stay with the work they love to do?

The knowledge and insight accumulated through decades of experience is a treasury from which regular withdrawals can be taken. Yes, younger men or women might do it better. But if none is available, what is lost by older people doing the job?

Isn't that why big employers already mentioned — McDonald's, Wal-Mart, Days Inn, Radio Shack, IBM, and others — have already started to reach out to older workers? There are not that many young people wanting to sign on for work which older people can do as well. Just as these corporations have grown to their mammoth, multinational size through staying on the right side of the marketing curve, so they have looked ahead in their human resources policies.

That's why the 21st century will see a turnaround in its estimate of what older people can do. The change will be forced on us by some needs not being filled by young people and by the ability of older men and women to do jobs that do not demand a physical effort they can no longer put forward.

And the workplace will not be the only one to feel that impact of the age revolution.

The astronomical salaries paid to major league sports stars is justified by their short "shelf life." After a few years of maximum physical effort they are used up, the body being said to go into decline after age 25. But what if the body is not needed as a priority? What if not many bright young men and women are clamoring to have their chance? When we join together the ability of older people to do a job and a smaller supply of young people looking for work, the sum is clear. More older people in the workplace. Retirement will be retired. Or at least delayed.

Even modified as a part-time lifestyle.

The threat of pension funds going into a tailspin is serious, yet not as sure and devastating a threat as it might be. The coming age revolution will not only give older people a new freedom, it will give society an injection of new life.

That boost will be imperative. As this century began, about 40% of Canadians were retiring before they turned 60 years of age. Taking that many people out of the work force without replacing them could have been critical, except that many are returning. Not always to their old job, or even their old industry, since many are striking out in a new direction they had hankered after for years. With a steady income assured from pensions and investments, they find themselves free at last — not to loaf, but to do work that had been an unfulfilled desire for years.

According to Statistics Canada about 32% of all Canadians still working at age 55 years or over are self-employed. They are people who created their own jobs, people who proved two things about elders at work. One is that elders can often hire themselves. And when they do, nobody else can fire them. But whether they go back to their old employer or launch out on their own, a growing trend is now clear: Elders are staying in the labor force, or returning to it. The coming age revolution has already started in the workplace, but its impact is being felt far beyond that: It is reaching as far as the corridors of power.

CHAPTER 4

Elders in Power

When the number of older people increases and the youth population declines, something like "Gray Power" has to appear.

The term itself was coined in the 20th century when elders began to organize and defend their interests. Whenever a delegation appeared on their behalf or a demonstration waved placards and shouted slogans in front of television cameras, it was dubbed "Gray Power." And it was more than media hype making a good story into a better one.

That it was a serious political force even in the late 20th century partially explains how so many entitlements for older people could become part of the social fabric. To be gray no longer meant to be weak. In the 21st century, to be gray will mean to be strong.

DAMN THE DEFICITS

Gray Power demonstrated this in the United States in 2003, when a Republican-controlled Congress passed legislation to assist older people with the cost of prescription drugs. What this would add to future deficits was well known, and its potential for financial ruin was spelled out. The demographics meant that increased entitlements were like an iceberg drifting in front of a ship's bow at sea. The number of low-income beneficiaries alone came to 10 million. And their number would escalate. The colossal sum of $88 billion in subsidies to maintain current employer-provided plans would be needed to ensure that people with this kind of private coverage would not lose it.

But these facts did not matter. Fiscally conservative Republicans were the proposal's strongest supporters, and critical Democrats were incensed only that the provisions for public support were not greater. What mattered to most on both sides was the growth of the older people's vote — and elections were just 12 months away. The time was politically right for what AARP (American Association of Retired Persons) could call the "largest expansion of Medicare since its creation in 1965." But old age entitlements have always been political. Why shouldn't they be in the 21st century?

SOCIAL SECURITY IS BORN

Old age entitlements might not have started at all in the United States if the economics of the 1930s had not made something like Social Security politically inescapable.

In 1933, a California physician named Francis Townshend found himself among the masses of unemployed Americans when he was dismissed from his public health position by a new city administration. The experience sensitized Dr. Townshend to the plight of his fellow citizens who, like himself, suddenly found themselves out of work and out of hope.

What bothered the doctor was the lack of a good explanation for this new phenomenon that denied all the assumptions the American people had held so long. People needed as many goods and services as ever, and people wanted to work as much as ever. Yet factories were closed, and lineups for jobs were long. It challenged all reason, especially when the country sank deeper and deeper into despair of ever finding a solution. That is, until Townshend hit on one.

He tried it out in diverse forms until his proposal for ending unemployment and depression both gelled into a formula that was so simple it seemed too good to be taken seriously. Townshend proposed paying every older American $200 a month on two conditions: he or she must not hold a job, and must spend all the money before the next month's check came. Putting all this cash into the economy each month would create all kinds of jobs which younger people would fill while their elders would enjoy a well deserved retirement. The plan was summed up in a neat slogan: "Youth for work and age for leisure." But where would the money for this new paradise come from?

Townshend proposed a federal sales tax until he was persuaded this would be hard on the lower-income people he wanted to help. Brushing aside that difficulty, the doctor soon won support of people across the country for what was called the Townshend Revolving Old Age Pension Plan. That support might have melted like winter snow under a spring sun, except that Townshend was joined by a partner that knew how to give a good idea legs that could carry it to Washington.

He was Robert Earl Clements, a California real estate broker, who brought organizational and promotional ability to the cause. Soon Clements had Townshend Plan supporters organized into over 300 local clubs across the country, each of their members pumped up regularly by the *Townshend National Weekly* with a circulation of 200,000 subscribers. They soon became a national movement, their meetings inspirational as well as organizational with such hymn-like songs as:

Onward Townshend soldiers,
Marching as to war,
With the Townshend banner
Going on before.
Our devoted leaders
Bid depression go;
Join them in the battle,
Help them fight the foe.

To many it seemed that a march on Washington could not be stopped. Yet it was stopped. Not by crushing it, but by replacing it with something that met the same need. Not as imaginatively daring as the Townshend Plan had proposed doing, but still acceptably. It would be adopted by Congress, approved by the president, and soon become part of the social fabric. It was Social Security.

Social Security offered middle-aged people future hope of an income when they reached retirement age. It would finance this income from payroll taxes to be paid by both employers and workers. As well, it would offer young people hope of employment by removing older people from the work force when they became eligible for benefits.

Although the Act was fiercely opposed by business throughout the 1936 presidential election campaign, it was one of the reasons Roosevelt swept the country. For the first time ordinary people could face the future without anxiety that they would eke out their last years in dependence on their families or welfare. It was not as exciting a hope as the Townshend Plan had supplied, but that lack may have even won Social Security greater support. Americans were not used to quick-fix schemes working. If Roosevelt's Social Security was low-keyed, that appealed to people whose expectations were as modest as their lifestyles.

What was significant was the rise of Gray Power to a strength that could create movements like Townshend's and motivate legislation like Roosevelt's. It had had precedents before in the case of United States Army veterans of the Civil War successfully pressing for pensions in the 1890s if they had reached an age when physical labor had become arduous. It had led to Alaska initiating a pension for destitute older workers, a precedent followed eventually by 35 states before the federal government took the lead in 1935 with Social Security. It had encouraged the agitation for retirement pensions for railroad workers so that senior men would take their pensions and not block the way of younger men. By the 1930s, Gray Power had become strong enough to be a major factor in a presidential election. Does it take a flight of the imagination to foresee how much impact it will make in the 21st century when the older generation has become a dominant part of the voting population?

NOT A YOUNG PERSON'S GAME

There is nothing about politics that must exclude older people from plunging in.

Winston Churchill was 66 when the British people turned to him to save the country from Nazi conquest in 1940. Most people thought he was finished, and probably he would have been if the greatest crisis in Britain's long history had not called him to the prime minister's office. Konrad Adenauer (1876–1967) was 76 when he was plucked from obscurity to lead Germany's recovery after the devastation of World

War II. It would not have happened otherwise because Adenauer had only been the mayor of Cologne. But he was one of the few German politicians who had no Nazi taint whatsoever. So the Allied powers put him at the head of Germany's reconstruction government. What a job der Alte did, doing it so well he was unbeatable at the polls. But he was not the only septuagenarian to win high office. Nelson Mandela was 75 when he was chosen the first president of a free South Africa.

Should we be surprised then if we see older men and women seeking office in the 21st century instead of assuming the calendar has disqualified them? It could look like the most obvious thing for an older person to do.

Someone like Maggie Kuhn showed elders could do it. When she was ordered to retire at age 65 from her Presbyterian Church of America headquarters staff job, Maggie reasoned that she was anything but too old to help people. Since she had been stirring up action for justice for years, why shouldn't she keep on doing it? If she could not do it for the church, she would do it on her own. And do it she did until she died in her 90th year.

With five friends in 1970, Maggie started the Consultation of Older and Younger Adults for Social Change. One of its objectives was to combat ageism, whether the discrimination was against the old or the young. Within their first year, the founding five expanded to one hundred members, and just the next year, they took that grabber of a name by which the movement is still known: Gray Panthers.

Then they teamed up with Ralph Nader's Retired Professional Action Group to add more people and more agenda. Gray Panthers were on their way to showing what Gray Power could mean — and not just for old people. One of their priorities was taking up any cause that would make life better for people as people, regardless of age.

In more than a quarter-century of intense campaigning, they championed health care, but not just as an elder issue. They declared it a human right. Their whole agenda became as broad as human need. It ranged across the entire social spectrum to comprehend nursing home reform, hearing aid regulation, international peace, political integrity, economic justice, jobs and workers rights and community safety. World affairs have not been ignored by politically oriented elders either.

In the crucial sector of peace in a warring world, a leading role was taken by a retired United States admiral. Gene LaRocque, at age 74, still led the Center for Defense Information, an organization he spearheaded as a way of keeping an eye on Pentagon spending. Himself a veteran of World War II, Korea and Vietnam, the admiral could not be labeled a peacenik, just a citizen concerned about "the growing influence of the military and industry," and determined that older citizens will get a bigger say.

ELDERS CAN LOBBY TOO

These social activists, however, are not unusual as an example of older people refusing to sit on the sidelines of the political game. One of the largest and most influential lobby organizations in the United States is the AARP (American Association of Retired People). It has 35 million members, all over 50 years of age, and two-thirds of them 65 years old or more. Each month, those millions of members all receive political bulletins alerting them to developments that could impinge on their lives, and urging them to advise their political representatives what elders are thinking. No other sector of the American public is better organized than this one, and no other sector votes in such massive numbers. The escalation of the elder population in the 21st century has to be a dominant feature of American politics.

What the farm vote used to mean, the elder vote will mean in the future. The decline of population in the one will be matched by its surging growth in the other. And in a democracy, politics are a numbers game. When those numbers are organized professionally, they gain power through research staffs, communication channels, experienced lobbyists, and organized campaigns. They cannot be ignored, and are taken seriously.

North of the U.S., in Canada, an organization called CARP ("Canada's Association for the Fifty-Plus") provides comparable services to its 400,000 members. These include representation of its members to both federal and provincial governments. It also communicates with the membership through a monthly magazine, and CARP keeps the country's decision makers aware that a major part of their constituency is over 65 years of age, with even more of it over 50.

In the 19th century, North American politics were determined by three R's — race, region, and religion. But in the 21st, those three elements will have to be joined by a fourth that is common to them all: age. And age is as influential as it was in the 20th century, and its impact will be just as massive in the 21st.

Does that mean something sinister? Something like a colossal gerontology lobby manipulating governments to provide more and more benefits for what Boomer Generation critics have called "greedy geezers"? No. Gray Power could try to work that way, but history shows there is little chance it will.

NO OLDSTERS' PARTY

On both sides of the Atlantic there have been Labor parties, Farmers' parties, Green parties. The politics of Canada's second largest province were dominated through the 1990s by a single party, the Parti Québécois, that was devoted to making that province into a sovereign country. For four years, the Bloc Québécois was the second largest party in the House of Commons and the Parti Québécois formed the provincial government for two terms. In the 2004 federal election, it trounced the governing Liberals in Quebec. So a special interest party can be viable.

In the United States, it is claimed that Ralph Nader's environmentalist candidacy for president may have taken enough votes from Al Gore to cost him the White House in 2000. At the state level, the Liberal Party of New York has often been a serious factor in elections because it could often swing enough votes either way to determine which Republican or Democrat would be elected governor of the state or mayor of New York.

So why shouldn't an older persons' party form itself early in the 21st century?

One reason is that people tend to stay in age what they were in youth. If they were supporters of a party for several decades, they usually do not shift their allegiance once they have passed 50 or 60 years of age.

Another reason may be that few people would find pleasure in belonging to something its rivals could label "the old folks' party."

Still a third reason is the wisdom that special interests have usually not served themselves best on their own, but by influencing whatever party is in power. Any government has to accommodate a diversity of interests, and regardless of what its label is, a government has to face the reality there are enough elder votes to elect it or defeat it. Gray Power is likely to remain what it is — a major influence on government that with time has so grown in size and scope it has to be respected.

That was why the United States presidential election of 2000 showed both major parties vying with each other to attract the votes of older citizens. The Republican Party Election Platform that year pointed to the danger of the Social Security fund running short of cash by 2015, and the income from payroll taxes being insufficient to cover current benefits. But conversely, the Republican platform in 2004 avoided such alarms. Instead, it assured voters that Social Security would remain unchanged for anyone then on it.

On the other side, the Democrats campaigned against raising the age of eligibility, advocated fairer provisions for widows, widowers and mothers, as well as offering a program called Retirement Savings Plus which would give people a voluntary, tax-free, personally controlled, privately managed way for couples to build a retirement fund up to $400,000. In addition, they stressed their commitment to securing a safe, affordable supply of prescription drugs for seniors, and their strong opposition to any form of privatizing Social Security.

The century thus began with older people's interests being better served by established parties competing with each other for Gray Power votes rather than losing them to a new party formed by older people who despaired of being taken seriously otherwise.

ELDERS IN OFFICE

But as an alternative, will we see legislatures filled by older people rather than younger? We are likely to see more elders run for office at all levels of government simply because there will be more of them. And also older men and women have already shown they can do the job as well as younger people.

The late Congressman Henry B. Gonzalez was still in Washington at age 82 — and undefeated at the polls. Why wouldn't he be when he gave his San Antonio district his total commitment? On a typical day, he arrived at the Hill shortly after seven o'clock in the morning, worked there all day and into the evening, and then he would go back to his apartment, have a sandwich, take a turn in the gym, and return to his office where he would work until midnight.

At 76 years old, Sophie Masloff was serving as mayor of Pittsburgh, a job she did well enough to hold for six years. It was also a job that had not been easy for her to get. The first time she ran, each of her four opponents raised her age as an issue because she was 72. But her age did not stop her. Instead she stopped her ageist rivals. She thus became not only the first woman mayor of the city, but also the first Jewish mayor — and even more unusual, the first grandmother to sit in the mayor's chair. And all this when she was over 70.

Stan Darling was first elected to Canada's Parliament from the Ontario riding of Parry Sound-Muskoka in 1972 when he was over 60, and held his seat through six elections without a defeat, retiring only in 1993 when he was in his 80s. During those years he built a national reputation for his advocating legislation against acid rain and was a factor in the international negotiations that led to the Clean Air Act. He drove home from Ottawa each weekend to attend constituency events, boasting that if even a dog fight was held anywhere in his vast Northern Ontario riding, he would be at it.

So why do we think politics is not an option for older people when the record shows how well they do at it?

In the 1990s, Judge Abraham Lincoln Marvitz was still senior judge of the United States district court at age 82. And 100 years earlier, William Ewart Gladstone formed his last cabinet as British prime minister in his 83rd year. In politics, as in anything else, age is irrelevant as a top priority. Only ability and character count that much, and they are ageless.

But since elders will represent a larger section of the public, they may form a large part of the legislatures at all levels of government. Shortly before Paul Martin was sworn in as Canada's prime minister in 2004 at age 64, he was asked by a reporter if he would seek re-election when he would be almost 70. The reporter's question represented an out of date 20th century prejudice. But Martin's answer expressed the 21st century attitude to elders in power. It was simply: "Why not?"

His answer takes on all the more meaning when we appreciate that despite the escalation of their numbers, older citizens have not sought — nor received — special representation in the inner councils of government. In addition to the usual departments of defense and agriculture, cabinets have often included members in charge of women's issues or youth issues but not elder issues. Governments have departments for veterans' affairs but not always older people's concerns. There is a reason for this, and it explains why the age revolution will not see that lack filled.

The age revolution does not mean older people will gain privilege. It will not seek special status for older people. Just the opposite. Its aim will be to break down the wall of division between older people and the rest of society. It will be to say "Enough!" when it faces all the usual assumptions about older people having special needs and deserving special treatment. The age revolution will demand that the ghettoization of elders be dumped on the garbage heap of outworn, unwelcome prejudices. Older people will take prominent places in government, but their leadership will aim at the common good.

Lobbies like AARP and CARP will represent elder interests legitimately just as other lobbies represent labor and business and a host of other causes that deserve a hearing. But elders in power will balance those concerns along with all the others so that society as a whole is served.

One of the outstanding prime ministers of the United Kingdom in the 20th century was a woman — Margaret Thatcher. She was so brilliant a leader she served longer than any other British prime minister in the 20th century. She was thus part of that century's gender revolution. Should it surprise anyone that in the 21st century, some elder could do the same?

Mrs. Thatcher had to blaze her own trail as the first woman to chair a British cabinet. And she did it so well that she won three elections in a row, something that no man had done in that century. Why should older men and women not be expected to do the same in the 21st?

True, they will need good health of mind and body. But wouldn't they need that if they were in their 40s or 50s as well?

STANDING UP FOR THEIR RIGHTS

But the age revolution will mean not only older men and women seeking office, winning elections and governing cities and countries. It will mean individuals refusing to act like the "little old ladies" or the "retiring" older men that age mythology has insisted they be.

In the city of Edmonton, the capital of Canada's western province of Alberta, and a hub of its oil and natural gas industry, lives a 69-year-old grandmother, Olga Friesen. Olga made the national news for a very unusual grandmotherly act. She announced she was ready to go to jail for a day rather than submit to what she saw as bullying by the city's government. Her offence was not clearing the sidewalk in front of her home after a snowfall. Fined $85 for this failure, she refused to pay it even though that made her liable to at least one day behind bars. In her defense she did not plead her age or her gender. She insisted that she was physically capable of doing it and she had three adult children living in Edmonton. She was just "mad as hell" at this city by-law and she wasn't going to take it any more. "I'm not too old to shovel my sidewalk," she stated. "I'm just too old to be bullied." Olga made her point. She was booked but spent only 20 minutes in custody.

Jim Krusic is another person who will not submit to other people's expectations of what older people should not do. He is still driving his own car at age 100, and he has been doing it since 1939 when he bought his first vehicle. But Jim is not unique, for in the Canadian province of Ontario despite a network of expressways filled with speeding cars and careening transports, there are 12 citizens over 100 years who still hold driver's licenses. Two of them are 102. Nine are 101. Jim is only the 12th-oldest driver in Ontario.

Should this be forbidden? Every time an older person is blamed for a motor accident, that question leaps into the minds of younger people who forget that the accident rate in their age group is far greater in percentage terms than it is among the older generation. In statistical terms, older people are not the threat on the roads that hard-driving younger people are, yet no opportunity to add a load of guilt to the shoulders of older drivers is missed. But the facts do not warrant it. Only stereotypical thinking supports it — but not for long.

In the 21st century there will simply be too many older people to draw an age limit for licensing. The social and economic impact would be too serious for older drivers to be forced off the road. If they were to be a small fraction of the population, perhaps they could go on being bullied (except for hardy individuals like Olga and Jim). But the "stats" show there are going to be just too many older people to be frozen out of buying and leasing vehicles which they will go on driving. And that is only one example of older people asserting their rights in the 21st century.

It was not easy for older people to gain a hearing for their grievances when the human rights codes historically excluded workers over 65 from charging employers with age discrimination. But when mandatory retirement withers away demographically, this barrier to legal redress will come down with it, and so will the forcefulness of the law's protection.

Although human rights commissions can deal with complaints by older men and women against their employers' discrimination and have boldly condemned all forms of age discrimination, their record has not shown a vigorous defense of older workers. In the 20th century it was easy for employers to find some rationalization for failing to give an older man or woman the promotion they deserved. They could not admit to being age-prejudiced, so they rationalized that the younger person had more qualifications, or that the older worker's performance was inferior. And so on and on. But the numbers will change that — more employers will be older; more job vacancies will threaten, and older workers will come into their own when they seek the defense of their rights by the law.

GRAY POWER CAN BE GOOD POWER

What older people obtained in the 20th century was not more self-seeking than what was gained by other segments of society. It also benefited all other segments of society by enabling older people to be financially independent consumers of goods and services produced by younger people. The ascension of older people to even greater political significance need not dilute that. Gray Power can serve the common good.

* * *

Gray Power will be the political consequence of the demographic shift from a young society to an aging one. In the 20th century, Gray Power led to programs such as Social Security and the 21st century began with "Pharmacare" legislation. In this century other issues of importance to older North Americans will gain significance as elders increasingly gain positions of power and as elder lobby groups become more influential.

CHAPTER 5

Elders in Health

O f the United States' nearly 300 million people, only one of them has been allowed to have his own army. Wherever he has gone, they have too. Not to protect him, only to cheer him on. They are "Arnie's Army" and for decades this devoted legion of Arnold Palmer fans has been one of the most appealing features of the golf scene. They supported their hero during the years he was winning no fewer than 61 golf championships on the PGA tour, and they are just as supportive now, following his retirement, when he continues to appear in tournaments. What makes him a model for everyone still?

Moving into his 70s has not weakened the combination of mastery and modesty that made Arnie a champion's champion among professional golfers, and a uniquely attractive hero to golfing fans. But there's more significance to Arnie's popularity still.

This perennial celebrity of a septuagenarian shows what the coming age revolution can mean to elder health. He is still playing better golf than most people half his age, and he is still drawing crowds as one of the great sports stars of all time. But that is not all.

He is also a successful entrepreneur, with a sporting goods manufacturing company, a golf course design practice, and a golf management business. All three enterprises remain part of his life at an age when the 20th-century ideal was to retire from work to pleasure as soon as a person could. In his 70s, as in his 20s, he is a person to watch. And that's the promise of the coming age revolution.

The assumption that growing older must mean growing weaker will be shown for what it is — a half truth. An older person usually cannot be as strong and agile in age as in youth. But in the 21st century, older people can be healthier and fitter than most people their age were in any previous time in history.

Like the four camping grannies of the Ontario town of Bracebridge. The oldest is in her upper 70s, the youngest in her mid-60s. But every summer, all four of them — Beth Black, Norma Bustard, Eileen Reville, and Mary Wilkins — are off camping. And it's *real* camping.

Like their 2004 tour of Yukon and Alaska: They caught their dinner in a rushing, northern river instead of ordering it in a restaurant, and cooked it over a fire they had built instead of on a range. They entertained themselves chatting with people they met instead of flicking the TV on, and then slept in a tent they had pitched in the open instead of a room they had rented in a motel. And by doing all this, they sent a silent message.

Their message is part of the coming age revolution. Older people can do what used to be thought good only for younger people.

In no aspect of life will the coming age revolution make a more dramatic change than health. There is a finitude to human existence that cannot be escaped. But its arrival can be delayed. As well, the time in between can be made quality time. That's the prospect this revolution opens to us.

We will continue to grow old. There's no other way to stay alive. But the coming age revolution will challenge the decrepitude that seemed for so long to be the inexorable fate of humanity. Three dynamics are already working their magic to add both years and vitality to older people.

One is the advance of the healing arts and sciences, and our expanding access to them. A second is improving our lifestyles personally and socially so that we can build our own health up through the years instead of wearing it down.

And a third is the chance for meaningful work to be done by older people. It will not be drudgery, it will be opportunity. The chance to add to elder health without a single pill being needed.

HEALING ARTS AND SCIENCES

When the telephone rang, I welcomed the voice at the other end. The voice of a man whose friendship I had enjoyed since school days. But I did not welcome the news he gave me.

He had been diagnosed with a type of cancer which could not be treated successfully, and he had already arranged his affairs with his family. But one thing was still on his mind. "Would you say a few words over this 'heathen' when the time comes?" he asked.

The time did come. Sadly I was privileged to fulfill his request at an impressive memorial service attended by so many family, friends, and admirers that they filled a large church. It was not difficult to find the words because Darrel McEwen's life had been a model for others.

He had been a member of "the greatest generation" in every way. A World War II veteran who went ashore on D-Day, he returned to graduate from university as a pharmacist. He then served a second time in the Canadian army, and later went into business, rising to an executive position. Yet he always put his wife, Marion, and their children first, even when it meant sacrificing promotions that would have eroded his family life.

But — and this is a big "but" — my having to say those "few words" did not come until years after that telephone call. During that extended time, he was able to have an almost full life through the help of medications pharmaceutical science had developed. He and his wife sold a house that was larger than they would ever need again, and they moved into an attractive condominium so they could both enjoy one another, as well as family and friends. He maintained his community interests which were many for a man who was primarily a "people person."

But weren't the medications just delaying the inevitable hour? Yes. That is all any treatment could have done. Or ever do. There is no way of avoiding the end indefinitely. But as the healing arts and sciences advance, we are given more ways of postponing it. And that is better than winning the lottery. Every added day is a bonus, a gift of life itself, something totally irreplaceable. Of all the advances the world gained in the 20th century, none added to humanity more than this one. It was a terrifying century for the slaughter of people but, ironically, an inspiring one for extending the lives of people who otherwise could have been cut down so much earlier. In the 21st century, no expectation can be greater than the prospect of still more progress in the healing arts and sciences.

We see it in the extension of life expectancy from what it was in 1900 to what it became by 2000. When the 20th century began, there were only 123,000 Americans aged 85 or more. At the century's end, the number had escalated to almost five million. Although the national population had quadrupled, the number of "old oldsters" had multiplied 50 times, enough to fill one of the largest cities in the country if one had been populated solely by people 85 years and older! And people that age did not need to say "game over." According to the medical journal *Geriatrics*, many persons who reached age 85 in 1997 could expect to live another 5.5. to 6.5 years.

Frail and sore as many of them are, the oldest sector of the American population has a survival potential this age group has never had before. At even mid-century, the percentage of persons expected to survive from birth to age 60 was only 52.3%. By 2000, it had soared to 83.6%. But that was not all. The health of older people had so improved that the fastest growing sector of the population were those 85 and over.

What a contrast with the early years of the republic when life expectancy was only 33 years for men and 35 for women. Health resources in the early 19th century were so limited that, for most people, being "old" began as they entered their 50s. Early America was not only a new country, it was a young one. No fewer than 45% of the people in a Connecticut city like Hartford were under age 20.

In the United Kingdom, the same aging trend has been followed. Life expectancy at birth is now 76 years for males, and 80 for females. But not so long ago, it was only a fraction of that. In 1891, just over seven percent of the population was 60 years of age or over. A hundred years later, one in five Britishers was in that category. The same trend is now found all over the developed world. At the start of the 21st century, over 12% of Australia's population was 65 years of age or more.

By 2030, one in four Canadians will be older than that. If not one new person were added to the population between now and then, Canada would have almost eight million elders just one generation from now. In the year 2000, this country held 3.8 million persons aged 65 and over — over 10% of its population. That was a 62% jump from what it had been in 1981, and the rate of elder growth was twice what it was among the rest of the population. But will this continue? According to Statistics Canada, it will escalate.

Has this progressive "graying" of the population across the developed world not been due to the fall in the fertility rate? And with that, proportionately fewer babies being born?

No. Not solely. It has also resulted from the mortality rate going into sharp decline as the century advanced. Due greatly to progress in the healing arts and sciences, people have been living longer and staying stronger. Throughout the 20th century that meant the steady advance in life expectancy which can be even longer in the 21st. And not just longer in time, but stronger in vitality.

People might still quote Shakespeare's "Ages of Man" with its frightening assessment of aging as the process of decay into nothingness — "sans eyes, sans teeth, sans taste, sans everything." But as the 20th century ended, people were not only adding years to their lives, many were adding quality to their time as well. Despite their years, they were "sans" scarcely anything.

Many nonagenarians can still read, drive, even shoot. Many "old, old" (that is, 85 plus) people go to their graves still with their own teeth, still able to enjoy a good meal. Shakespeare was right in his time, but not now — at least, not for everyone.

True, aging is still a process of decline. Lean body mass diminishes. So does bone density. Digestive secretions are reduced too. The march of time leaves its road marks on the face and hands. But that is no longer the whole story.

Nutrition alone is a factor in revolutionizing health for older people. Foods rich in iron and calcium as well as low in salt can reinforce the aging body. Zinc-containing foods can assist that body to heal some of the wounds that so easily beset elders. Vitamin E foods — such as whole grains, peanuts, vegetable oil — can give it new strength.

Drinking enough water — five to eight glasses a day — can relieve stress on the kidneys.

At one time, these health suggestions were often taken only by the few ready to go against the stream of conventional living. They were written off as "fitness freaks" or "health nuts." But as the 21st century begins, they are becoming the norm. By the time the "Boomers" become elders, people will be staying healthy by eating healthy.

Although there remains no way of avoiding a final end, there have emerged inspiring ways not only to push that end back, but to do it with enough vigor to turn those added years into a time of achievement. Life is now a game where the goal posts can be moved.

As a result, age can cease to be an acceptably solo reason for diagnosing a person's condition and leaving it at that, as though no other explanation is needed than a trite, "You are getting on, you know."

As Dr. Hans Selye wrote in *The Stress of Life,* "Among my autopsies I have never seen a man who died of old age . . . We invariably die because one vital part has worn out too early in proportion to the rest of the body."

Science has already shown that when a body part can be replaced (such as a new heart) or assisted (such as with bypass surgery) life can go on. Not forever, it's true. But every added year can be a bonus. And that is not the whole story.

Through much of the 20th century, life expectancy's growth was due to the decline of infant mortality rates. Then it advanced in the latter part of the century partly through progress in geriatrics.

It took some time, and even more effort, to establish geriatrics in medicine. It demanded commitment by medical pioneers ready to explore a new dimension of the healing sciences. One of them was a British woman. In 1935, Dr. Marjorie Warren discovered older people in the British "Poor Law Infirmaries" were not being treated actively because the prevalent staff attitude was: "At their age, what's the use?"

Dr. Warren thought that question should have an answer. As deputy superintendent of the West Middlesex County Hospital, London, she was responsible for 700 mostly bed-bound patients for whom little or no effort was being made to release them from that bondage. To compound the problem, she found the patients were giving up on themselves, as though an unseen power had decreed: "It's time to say,

'Goodbye.'" So Dr. Warren set about correcting this human write-off.

It took determination because an implicitly ageist attitude still prevailed in the mind of officialdom. It was implied even in the otherwise reforming 1942 Beveridge Report on social insurance. That generally progressive document argued it would be "dangerous" to launch elder care programs until "all other vital needs" had been met. That was "bureaucratese" for saying that old people should have no priority at all.

But determination was a quality Dr. Warren had. Through the efforts of pioneering physicians such as she, a whole province of medical science was encouraged to expand. Both professionals and the public now recognize that elders can be healthy, and that they should therefore be treated with what they need to pursue healthy lives.

From those early days, geriatrics has evolved as a respected part of medicine. Its study is now included in the curricula of medical schools as part of what any physician should know. Journals are published to keep physicians up to date on what can be done for older patients. Yes, some physicians may still assume an adequate diagnosis has been made by commenting, "It's just your age. " But that no longer needs to be accepted as a definitive, scientific statement. Geriatrics has shown sickness is not solely a matter of chronology.

An 80-year-old lady demonstrated this when she consulted her doctor about a very sore knee. His response disappointed her. Instead of explaining the cause and offering the hoped-for treatment, he was content to advise the lady that the problem was her age. As he put it, her sore knee was 80 years old. As though that should be a total explanation. But if he thought that would send her away content, he was mistaken. In her mind, it was not a scientifically verifiable diagnosis at all. So she protested: "But doctor, my other knee is also 80 years old. And it isn't sore."

Although that physician is still not unique in his ageist attitude, medicine as a science has moved beyond ageism. True, some diseases and conditions are more often found among older people than younger. Yet age itself is not the all-sufficient cause. More important, age need not prevent seeking a cure. Life expectancy has surged ahead because medical science has assumed cures can be found regardless of age, even when a disease prevails chiefly among older people.

Although Alzheimer's disease is more often found in persons over 60 years of age and among half the men and women aged 85 or older, the study of over 800 brains convinced researchers Hake and Eva Braak, in 1991, that this disease's "tangle related lesions appear in people as young as twenty." They established six stages of the disease and concluded it may take 50 years or more for Alzheimer's to develop, but it is not an inevitable consequence of that aging.

Younger people may be afflicted by Alzheimer's, and older people may escape it. The cause is not time itself. Some assert it may be due to lifestyle, including faulty nutrition. So, whether people are dealing with a sore knee or Alzheimer's, it is not enough to shrug the challenge off with ageist passivity.

That does not mean time is medically irrelevant. It does mean, so geriatrics has established, that time is not an adequate explanation on its own. The pursuit of healing for all people — old as well as young — remains the motivation for all healing sciences.

This is also a premise of the coming age revolution, and we can expect it to be fulfilled because science, by definition, is progressive. So elders can look to this century as a time when the boundaries of health will be pushed back further than humanity has ever known.

The march to this tomorrow has already begun. One evidence of its progress is the astounding increase in the number of people living to advanced ages. Their longevity cannot be explained entirely in terms of medical science, but many now living would have long been dead but for the discoveries found in laboratories, developed by pharmaceutical companies, and prescribed by physicians.

And the march is not over. Overwhelming possibilities are becoming conceivable through efforts like the U.S. Human Genome Project. Launched in 1990 by the United States government, its aims were to identify the approximately 30,000 genes in the human DNA, then to comprehend the three billion chemical base pairs that comprise the DNA, and to share this information for the common good so that people can be cured of the many now-incurable diseases.

By using this knowledge to develop radically new and effective treatments for diseases and conditions that have been holding people in their grip so long, knowledge about not only human, but also nonhuman organic life can open up whole new provinces of health care. There is no need to assume that something for which no cure has yet been known must remain inexorably powerful over us forever. Equally, there is no need to assume that because people could be worn out at a certain age in times past, that age must be the beginning of the end in the future.

These so-called "old old" persons — that is, men and women aged 85 or more — may hold the secret to a longer lifespan for the rest of the population. If the explanation for their longevity were found to be genetic, it would be conceivable for research to find the gene for long life. Science could then develop a drug that could act on us the way that gene acts on those who hold it. It would be a longevity pill, and it would enable older people to fight illness more strongly and to respond to treatment more readily. Far out? Of course. Yet conceivable. And more important, potentially possible.

As well, the study of centenarians is teaching us lessons about extending our lives with quality time. The coming age revolution not only means that many people will live longer, it also means they will live stronger.

In a study based on the lives of 12,000 men and women, each aged 100 or more, called *The Centenarians: The New Generation,* Bella Boon Beard made this extraordinary claim:

"An idea that old age is synonymous with helplessness and inactivity must be revised in the light of these case histories of centenarians. Almost any activity pursued by a man can be continued past his 100th birthday."

She found centenarians who were doing gymnastics. Riding horseback. Driving their own cars. Looking after gardens. Practicing yoga. Chopping wood. And most common of all, walking. One was even riding his motorcycle regularly!

Mental activity was found to be not closed off at 100 either. And not just among aging Nobel Prize laureates. At Chattanooga, Tennessee, Mary Walker showed the way by learning to read and write at 100. Impossible? By the time she was 103, she was reading the Bible and writing her own letters!

Some were maintaining themselves at paid work. Others were performing volunteer jobs. Still others were attending church and community groups regularly. Twenty were in *Who's Who in America*. Some were still preaching, teaching, writing, painting.

None of which means there will be no weakness, sickness, pain, discomfort, or misery for the very aged. What these centenarian examples mean is that what has been the possibility for a few can become the experience of the many. And would that not be revolutionary?

Yet it need not be all the revolution that elders will enjoy in health. Along with these almost superhuman advances in the healing arts and sciences, the coming age revolution will result from a change in lifestyle by elders.

LIFESTYLE CHANGES

In the 21st century, older people can live longer and stronger not only because of pharmaceuticals, transplants, and therapies — marvels though they are. Living fitter lives has also started to extend our time on earth and to make it quality time. In the 21st century the coming age revolution can redefine what the term "old" means because it will encourage a healthier way to live. The change has already begun.

Wherever one turned as the 20th century ended, one could see this change in process. Tobacco use had plummeted across the developed world because of the cancer threat. At mid-20th century, smoking had been the smart thing to do. But now? Diehard smokers have to huddle together outside as temporary outcasts who must brave even the winter cold if they want to smoke. And that is only one facet in the lifestyle change that is part of the age revolution.

Hard liquor has been displaced as the alcoholic drink of choice in favor of beer and wine among younger people. Fat is on its way out of even fast food eateries where cheeseburgers have had to give pride of place on the menu to salads. Salt is becoming so much a "no no" that supermarket shelves carry many foods labeled "low salt" or "salt free."

Although none of this means older people will not remain prone to serious diseases, it does mean many more will escape them, and more will cope with them.

It is true that increased longevity has the downside of our becoming vulnerable to diseases we might not have suffered in shorter lives, but healthy lifestyles can mean we are better equipped to meet the enemy. Diabetes, for example, is such a hazard of aging that over half the 16 million Americans who suffer diabetes are more than 60 years of age. But a healthy lifestyle — including physical exercise and a nutritional diet — can help many cope with it. According to one study of Type 2 diabetes reported in *The New England Journal of Medicine,* "obesity and weight gain greatly increase the risk." Other factors are also lifestyle features: cigarette smoking, low-fiber diet, and specific dietary acids. Powerful as diabetes is, it no longer needs to mean the hostile takeover of an older person's life. Lifestyle can withstand it, and not just diabetes.

When 80% of fatalities due to heart disease are found among people aged 65 or older, the threat of coronaries has to be a constant for elders. But older people can take some precautions that will reduce that threat. High blood pressure puts a strain on the heart, which can be relieved by dieting and exercising. Any tobacco use is aiding and abetting an enemy that is already too powerful.

This applies also to strokes, which are the third most common cause of death. Although young people can suffer them too, strokes are found more often among elders. The danger of stroke is reported to double for each decade after age 55. But the healthier lifestyles of the age revolution can reduce this vulnerability. A person cannot decide not to have a stroke, but people can choose not to use cigarettes, not to overeat, not to indulge in anything that promotes hypertension.

When the 20th century began it was still fashionable for businessmen to be corpulent. A paunch was often called a "corporation." It symbolized how its owner also owned other assets. By century's end, however, a simpler lifestyle was gaining a credibility that can escalate in the century to come. For many, running and weightlifting at midday were taking the place of eating and drinking a two-cocktail business lunch.

Health does not depend just on the years people have lived. Nor does it depend on being young. We can abandon the presupposition that once we have reached a certain point in time, we should ready ourselves to hear a "game over" whistle blow. With the right lifestyle, the odds of living longer and stronger go up. But what makes that a revolution?

The revolution is in the mind. More people believe it at the start of the 21st century than did at the start of the 20th. We no longer have to believe that in the fourth quarter of the game, we have to become losers, since we have too many examples of the opposite. Some of them are not only models, they're marvels.

The founders and organizers of events like the National Seniors Games and the San Diego Senior Olympics have not assumed fitness comes from oldsters cheering on youthful athletic superstars. They have shaped programs with room for hundreds of participants old enough to be called "senior citizens." Each one has been proof that to be past 50 or 60 years of age need not eliminate you from serious athletics.

Founded in 1988, the San Diego Senior Sports Festival encourages older men and women to abandon the assumption that sports participation is for the young only. It has aimed at motivating older people to prioritize physical fitness as their key to good health, and the spin-off from all this promotion of fitness became colossal by the end of the 20th century.

By the time the new century started, physical fitness for elders had become an industry. Private gyms opened in neighborhoods and staff members were on hand to counsel people about how to work out safely. Their patrons included not only middle-aged aspirants, but "wannabe healthy" elders. Gray heads jogged around tracks with dark-haired youths, "raced" each other side by side on stationary bicycles, and sweated it out on treadmills. And all of this exposed the prejudice that aging means "weakness."

When elders can see someone like Jack Nicklaus pass the 60-year mark and still enter tournaments until he was 65 as well as run his own golf business, they know they have no good excuse to let themselves go physically or mentally. The "Golden Bear" has been called the greatest golfer of all time, and the record books show that to be correct. Nicklaus has won more tournament championships than anyone else in the world, and he has made himself a corporate champion by operating his own golf business. Best of all, his greatness is not behind him.

Obviously few people can shine as Nicklaus does. But that has nothing to do with their growing older. When was it in their younger years that they could command the attention he does as he grows older? The answer is not the point. What matters is that more elders are following the Nicklaus example of living healthy.

It's why an organization like AARP includes sport in its complex program. Its 20th-century program may have focused on very important but still physically passive services, such as insurance. But AARP began this century with a triathlon for people 50 or more in age. The event, staged at several strategic centers across the United States, from New York to Honolulu, included a 500-meter swim, a 20-kilometer bike ride, and a five-kilometer run or walk.

The New York Road Runners, a volunteer organization with a uniquely Manhattan-style program, has been able to recruit people of all ages for their one-of-a-kind athletic endeavor: running up the stairs inside the Empire State Building. A young Australian, Paul Crake, may have needed only nine minutes and 33 seconds to run up the 86 floors, but that impressive record took nothing away from contestants such as Lance Battari, a New Jersey engineer, who went all the way to the top at age 53. Yet at that age, he seemed only a stripling compared to the oldest runner. Chico Scimone, an Italian pianist, was able to meet the Empire State's challenge at an unbelievable 91 years of age for his 13th time at completing the distance.

Does Chico defy belief? Some time soon, thumb through a copy of *The Guinness Book of Records,* and see how it seems like a trip through fantasy land. Except that it is 100% fact.

A Japanese man, Shuhechugo Izumi, not only lived 120 years and 237 days from 1865 to 1986, he worked until he was 105. Here's a list of "the oldest . . . " according to *Guinness.* It's enough to deny you and me the right ever to say we are too old to try something.

Oldest Driver: Layne Hall, of Silver Creek, NJ, was issued a license at 109.

Oldest Air Pilot: Burnett Patten, of Victoria, Australia, was qualified at age 80.

Oldest Parachutist: Hildegarde Ferrara jumped in Hawaii when she was 99.

Oldest Olympic Medalist: Oscar Swahm at age 72.

Oldest Athlete: Baba Joguder Singh threw the discus at 105.

Oldest Bridegroom: Harry Stevens, an Australian, was married at 103.

Oldest Bride: Minnie Munro was married at 102 to a groom aged 83.

Oldest Anniversary: Joseph and Annie Jarvis celebrated 79 years together.

No, the age revolution will not mean thousands of older people scaling skyscrapers. But the 21st century can see more people like Chico. That, however, may not be its most important influence on people's lives.

WORKING FOR GOOD HEALTH

To enjoy complete wholeness, people need peace of mind as well as fitness of body. Despite the familiar picture of the aged being calm, even serene, that has not been the good fortune of all older people in the past.

Yet increasing the number of elders who enjoy it will be one of the age revolution's major thrusts. It needs to be. Mental and emotional traumas have been the fate of living too long for elders who have been condemned to years of idleness.

Has this been one of the reasons for suicide growing faster among people 85 and older than any younger age category? Just when they could have been expected to exemplify a sage and quiet life, many may have found they had no salvation in this world and should get out of it.

Older Americans, who now represent 13% of the population, also equal 20% of the suicides. Most of them — 81% — are men. According to Dr. Mark Rosenberg, of the National Center for Injury Prevention and Control, U.S. Department of Health and Human Services, three factors may explain this tragic development.

1. Change

We all need stability. The secure feeling of living with the familiar. But retirement can force that on people beyond their capacity for looking at the same faces. Hearing the same stories. Looking at the same four walls. That's what is behind the wife's complaint about her retired husband: "I married him for better or for worse. But not for lunch."

Just "going to work" offers something that the stay-at-home elder does not always get. It's a change. Even the trip with all its hassles — be it by commuter expressway or urban subway — gives a person something else to think about. A car is now equipped almost like a home. It means a commuter can listen to favorite music. Keep up with the news. Chat with passengers. All in the comfort of air conditioning.

Same on the trip back. But now with new memories of the day instead of old ones of years ago. Plus new problems solved. Tasks performed. People met. Yes, it could have been a hard day. But the trip home means retiring in a different way. Now home is itself a change.

Ennui, boredom, meaninglessness were long ago cited by industrial psychologists as a social problem modern workers faced because of the dehumanizing effect of mass production methods. But the solution did not lie in a retirement that just took them out of the workplace altogether. People still needed change, something that just going to work had given. Something that just staying home took away.

The coming age revolution's return to the workplace can meet that need. Older people will still want to play golf, take trips, spend time in the sunshine. But flexible retirement arrangements that permit people to work so many hours a day, so many days a week, or so many months a year can give them the balance which full retirement can deny.

That's one reason some companies already have no trouble filling their job banks with pensioners who want to work part-time. On the company's side, it makes sense because these people know the setup already. On the individual's side, it's an opportunity for not only more income, but a change too. The coming age revolution will make that more the norm than the unusual. The trend is already in place.

The fastest growing segment of the work force is already people 55 years or older. According to the U.S. Bureau of Labor, other age groups are dropping but this older one is escalating. By 2010, an estimated 26.6 million Americans 55 years or older will be on the job, an increase of 46% since the start of the century. When we recall how, in the 1990s, early retirement was considered "First Prize" for reaching age 55, this shift is nothing short of an age revolution. But what does it have to do with mental health?

It may not help with clinical depression, the kind that can ensue from vascular changes in the brain, or other medical causes. But it can help a lot with just plain boredom.

Armed forces personnel know that when a unit has nothing much to do, trouble can start. The officers know it too. So they contrive field exercises — training programs, maneuvers, almost anything to keep everyone busy at something different. It may be just a routine march five miles from camp and back. But it's a change. Soldiers need it. So do pensioners. Just as much. The coming age revolution means more will be getting it, plus something just as vital.

2. Togetherness

Most of our lives, we not only go to work, we work with other people. The job is not only a task, it's a fellowship, a team experience. A way of meeting our basic human need for society, for being part of one another.

Respect for that in the workplace is found wherever there is good management. A good boss knows that people work better when they have a sense of togetherness. It means feeling they are accepted by others. It means they can share interests and objectives. Going to work then means more than making a living. It means having a life.

But when retirement brings that to an end after decades of enjoying it, a great vacancy yawns in front of a person. It can be filled partially by clubs like Probus (an acronym for Professional and Business) that have expanded on three continents because they offer retired and semi-retired people a chance for fellowship without demands for fundraising or service.

The vacuum can be filled by fun with friends too. That partially explains the explosion of new golf courses. It can be filled also by making common cause with like-minded men and women. Like Habitat for Humanity's immeasurably inspiring service in building homes for lower income people.

But commendable as they are, these efforts do not meet everyone's need. Some people also prize the psychological lift they feel when they are still earning. If pressed in debate, they would agree that an unpaid volunteer is just as much "on the job" as they are, yet they still relish the pleasure one man was obviously tasting when he asked me: "How many people do you know who are still getting a pay check at 75?" Many older people want jobs as their way of going where people are.

The coming age revolution will do that with its return to the workplace. The 21st century will still have its clubs, its fun and its projects, but it will offer something else, something basic to enjoying a full humanity.

3. Achievement

Achievement will be an antidote to the inner emptiness that older people often suffer. Work not only means change and fellowship, it also offers opportunities for success. And that's a human need too. No school child is too young to experience it. That may be why I can still remember my Grade One teacher stamping a red star on the tree I had drawn with a black crayon during my first day in her class.

"Why did Miss Mowat do that?" I asked my mother when I showed her my paper at home. She beamed with maternal pride as she told me the star meant I had drawn a good picture of a tree. I beamed too. At six years, I did not know the word "achievement." But I now knew the positive feeling it could inspire. It was a good one. Good for young children and just as good for older people. But not always easy to find.

It may seem easier if one has a craft, such as writing. But writers must have readers to feel complete, so they must be published and to do so they necessarily interact with the outside business world and the public. To have a truly complete sense of achievement, most people have to do work which fills a need some other people have.

The work may be greeting customers as they enter the stores of the world's largest retailer. It may be reorganizing the finances of a Big Three auto company, or looking after a former boss when his assistant is on maternity leave. But at the end of the day, a person can feel it was a good day. Because something good was achieved.

Going back to work will not treat the kind of depression that needs professional care. But it can relieve and — more important — prevent some of the factors that drive older people's spirits down, down, down. The coming age revolution will help older people live longer and stronger than many of them could have by wallowing in the mistaken luxury of having nothing to do for the rest of their lives.

The late Tom Wardle was living proof of that. As a young man in 1938, Tom started a wholesale gift and souvenir business. Almost seven decades later, he was still operating it. He had always had family help. His wife Inez kept the business going through World War II while Tom served in the Canadian Air Force. She was right into it also in the years that followed when her extroverted husband chaired the Toronto Board of Education, was an alderman on City Council, and a member of the

Ontario Legislature. But Tom, during all those years, worked at the family firm every day no matter what his community service demanded.

In the latter years, he had his son, also named Tom, at his side too. Together they traveled through southern Africa and to Hong Kong to buy specialty products they brought back for their customers. Back home, they set out across the world's second largest country to market their wares to clients who operated souvenir stores at all the major tourist centers.

When they were not on the road, they ran their office and warehouse, hiring men and women they knew for years to parcel and ship their goods across the country. What was so unusual or impressive about that?

Maybe nothing, except that Tom was on the job until he was 90 years old, even having suffered heart attacks and strokes. He would have had reason to take up permanent residence in a retirement home's easy chair and make the TV guide his only agenda. But neither age nor illness stopped him. Having a healthy, willing, and able son to be his chief operating officer was an obvious reason why this was possible. But was it the whole reason?

Didn't Tom find his life healthier just because he could still do work he had done most of his life? He was able to give his partner the benefit of his long experience and he was still a part of the action. He got out of the house and spent the day in the office, chatting with his longtime employees and looking after his old customers. He even made a sale to a purely social visitor like me.

When older people work, they share in something potentially therapeutic. Few older people are unaware of being less useful — even useless — nor insensitive to the pain that can bring. Just knowing that one is helping some other person can mean a lot to improve one's mental health.

That's why the coming age revolution will offer the greatest benefit package older people have ever enjoyed.

People will be able to look forward to aging with health in this century. Not everyone will run in competition. But increased millions will remain physically active. Like the octogenarian woman who told me she was still golfing most days: "I don't drive very far. But I shoot straight. And I putt well."

Millions will copy another 80-plus woman — my wife's cousin, Doris Simington — who goes to Florida every winter regardless of what the health insurance costs. But not just to sit in the sun. She swims three times a day. Plays bridge two afternoons. Goes dancing two nights a week.

The coming age revolution will not rule out older people suffering disease, debilitation, and death, those three dark horses that have always stalked elders. But the revolution will rule out our assuming that aging must mean to us what it meant to an ancient Hebrew writer. For him, aging was something to dread. Something so agonizing that he warned young readers of their inescapably dark future in these metaphors of decline:

> [T]he years draw near when the keeper of the house *(arms and hands)*,
> will tremble, and the strong men *(legs)* are bent,
> and the grinders *(teeth)* cease because they are few,
> and those that look through the windows *(eyes)* are dimmed,
> and the doors *(ears)* on the streets shall be shut
> (Ecclesiastes 12:1–4)

Will we still risk all of that? Yes. But only risk it. More and more people will put it off. The night will come as it always has. Yet the age revolution will mean the day lasts longer than it ever has before. Admittedly that extra daylight can demand a price. It can be a new vulnerability that elders have not had to suffer before.

THE FLIP SIDE

Before compact discs and cassette tapes eliminated vinyl records from the music scene, people had to make the most of a two-sided record by turning it over to play what was called the flip side. Revolutions too have their flip side. They bring new opportunity to some, but disaster to others. Even when revolutions are achieving their just goals.

For instance, many bright young white men found that the race and gender revolutions of the 20th century meant reduced job possibilities for them as a result of affirmative action programs. There's a flip side to what the age revolution can mean to the health of older people, too.

Each year means another chance of being overtaken by one of the enemies that will not stop their pursuit just because some people are running faster. Although these diseases are not caused by age itself, the chance of one reaching into a person's life can escalate with time. The longer we live the greater the risk that we will succumb to one of them.

So the age revolution will mean not only living longer and stronger. It will mean more people running more risk of suffering more illnesses than ever, simply because living longer means that the enemy that did not strike yesterday may hit today. Or tomorrow. This paradox will not deny the gains of the revolution. It will be the logical result of our being on earth longer. And with that consequence, the flip side will mean yet one more development.

More resources, personal and national, may go to health care than to any other sector of the economy. More people will work in health care services than ever before. Will that be sustainable though? That's usually the first critical question, but it doesn't have to be.

Health care need not be only a threat. It can also mean an opportunity. Yes, the survival of more people through more years will cost big money. But just as the telecommunications revolution of the late 20th century brought new prosperity as well as new costs, so this flip side of the age revolution may produce more dollars than it consumes.

Whole new industries are already on the scene because we are becoming an aging society. Let's think of one small example that provides a straw to show us where the wind is blowing.

Canes went out of fashion not long after World War I as part of a well-dressed man's street outfit. Now they're "in" for men and women who need some help with painfully arthritic knees or an uncertain sense of balance. One afternoon at a busy intersection just two blocks from my Toronto home, I counted seven people using canes to make their way across the street while the traffic light was green. And that is but one small way that disabilities are creating new lifestyles which in turn create new markets.

A superstore can now provide shopping scooters specially designed for people who find themselves challenged by the extended aisles they must walk. Reserved parking spaces for disabled drivers are commonplace in shopping malls. The age revolution is already making disability less a reason to withdraw from society than it was for so long.

Marketing itself is being geared to two kinds of people who find it difficult to prepare meals in the traditional way. Some are customers who are too busy with their daily work to shop and cook the way their parents did. The others are people too incapacitated to try cooking meals for themselves every day. For both kinds, packaged foods have been so improved in variety and quality that both younger and older people can get their meals ready with minimal effort. And those are not all the changes that are being made.

A person need not actually go near a store. Some stores are providing shopping and delivery services which will take a customer's order over the telephone, fill it, and bring it to the door, and meals are often ordered now from neighborhood restaurants.

And those developments are only examples of how aging means a new market in parts of the economy.

By mid-century, it is estimated that half the United States' gross domestic product may be devoted to health care in all its varied forms. As a prediction, that is also an invitation to react with dread. "Can we afford it?" is a typical question that implies a negative answer. Before assuming the answer has to be "No," however, let's examine what this development can create for the economy. We will find it will not be only problems. It can mean "jobs, jobs, jobs."

If health care becomes as dominant a part of the scene as this prediction warns us, pharmaceuticals may forge ahead of defense industries in research, production, and distribution. Add to that all the therapy service agencies — hospitals, convalescent centers, nursing homes, assisted living communities, hospices — plus the training and research facilities that back them up, and we have only just begun to make up a list of services that an aging population may need.

Home care will be needed so that fewer older people will have to enter institutions, plus the renovation of homes to make them "friendly" for people who do not walk easily, or cannot reach high shelves, or cannot climb stairs, or use an ordinary bathtub. And reconstruction will also be demanded if public transit stations are to be fully accessible to older people.

As well, middle-aged sons or daughters may arrange medical leave or "flex hours" so that they can devote time to caring for aged parents.

Some estimate that such family members might spend more years on caring for aged parents than they gave to rearing children.

Yes, the "shopping list" seems endless. But not hopeless.

Every change that this trend involves is an economic opportunity. When we question the sustainability of health care for a graying world, we forget that question could have been asked about every economic change that has ever claimed dominance. Automobiles, for example. Making them, maintaining them, servicing them, parking them, selling them, reselling them. Cars not only provide transportation for people, they also mean work for millions, and that can be just as true with health care. It will be an industry that not only consumes wealth but also creates it.

Every health worker will be a customer for other sectors of the economy. Everyone will be taxpayer. Everyone will be a job creator. The economy has always adjusted to new needs and prospered from meeting them. Must it be inconceivable that the problems of an aging population will be balanced by the opportunities their needs will create?

The flip side of this revolution does not have to be only downside, since its challenges can be turned into creations. Even aging itself can be.

LIFE'S GREATEST GIFT

To people convinced of the cliché that nothing matters more than health, growing older has often seemed a threat. A rapidly aging population has been viewed almost as a pandemic crisis. This was because in the past, "old" had to mean "weak." Aging had to equal failing. But already elders are showing the world that adding years does not have to mean subtracting health. That trend can escalate. It can generate people whose strength will approximate their years. Yes, they will grow old, but not just old — they will grow better, especially when they enjoy not only health, but wealth, too.

* * *

Instead of age being equated with debilitation, it can be a time of active participation. The 21st century will mean dropping the age prejudice that to be old means to be weak. Several factors tell us the 21st century will see this change happen:

· Advances in healing arts and sciences that promise longer life expectancy.

- Healthy living lifestyle choices will assist in the life expectancy increase and the quality of that life.

- Remaining in the work force will contribute to elders' physical and mental health significantly.

CHAPTER 6

Elders in the Money

In 1965, Martin Luther King (1929–68) turned from civil rights in the American south to economic justice in the north as the focus of his crusade for African-Americans. This change of direction was rationalized with a folksy, down-home argument: "What's the use of having the right to sit at the same lunch counter as white people if you don't have the money to pay for a hamburger?"

King was right. Civil rights could confer only so much freedom. Economic justice had to be added before people could be free to live a fully human existence. And that's just as valid when the issue is age instead of race.

That's why the coming age revolution will enhance the economic potential of older people. Gone will be the advice that old age must be a time for scaling down, for reducing one's lifestyle. For learning to live on a fraction of the income people had when they were in the work force. Instead of learning to live on 60% of one's working days' income, it will be possible for elders to go on enjoying 100%.

People will stop assuming that their adult children or some younger advisor should manage an elder's finances, or that elders should passively accept their earning years have come to an end, and there's nothing they can do about it. Changing all that will be one of the most beneficial advances of the coming age revolution. Why will it be that important?

The concept that freedom is the objective of revolution applies to elders in their handling of money. The coming age revolution will mean older people gaining more opportunity for financial freedom.

For a fully human life, this freedom is a must. When elders depend financially on others, no matter how ready, willing, and able those others are, elders are not fully their own, sometimes pathetically so.

In her classic *Old Age,* Simone de Beauvoir (1908–86) relayed a Grimm Brothers story about a German peasant ordering his father to sit by himself at meals instead of at the family table. The older man thus was obliged to eat from a wooden trough placed in a corner of the kitchen. Why? This degradation was demanded because he did not eat with the fastidiousness the son expected. His hands shook enough for him to drop food on the floor.

Not long after debasing his father this way, the peasant found his son playing with wooden boards in an attempt to join them together like the trough he had seen his grandfather using. When the peasant asked the boy why he was making it, he was shocked to hear his son say: "It's for you when you are old." The message was clear. The point was made. The grandfather was restored to the dining table at once.

Yes, it's a soul searching, heartbreaking story. But it contains a germ of inescapable reality. It makes the point no elder will ignore in the coming age revolution. To be fully free, one must be economically independent.

High on the coming age revolution's agenda, then, are ways for older people to succeed with their wealth. Acquiring it. Managing it. Expanding it.

But did de Beauvoir go too far in claiming that "for the last 15 or 20 years of life, a man [is] no more than a reject, a piece of scrap"? Maybe. But she did not go too far if she was speaking about older people who lack the means to be financially free.

Although acquiring money often finds itself put under an ethical cloud, it is too basic to a fully human existence to be ignored, denigrated, or denied. As physical creatures in a material world, people need money for a full life.

People make a serious mistake if they speak of money as something to which we can and should be indifferent. It is a mistake because it demands our shutting out a huge block of reality. On its own, money means just pieces of paper. Pieces of metal. Pieces of plastic. But in the hands of men and women, money can become an instrument of freedom.

Money means being free to live where an older person wants to live instead of where relatives or the state provide. It means satisfying one's desires — be it for a new coat or an ocean cruise — instead of waiting for someone else's charity. It can open the door to health by enabling a man or woman to obtain the right medical care, or even create a chance for personal enhancement by paying for studies that have been long delayed but for which there is now time, as long as a person can pay the price for them. But isn't that all unrestrained selfishness? It can also mean an opportunity to help others, such as paying the cost of a grandchild's education, or opening a door of opportunity for a Third World youth.

Most important of all to a person's humanity, money provides freedom to choose. Older people who are financially independent have a freedom denied anyone else. So the age revolution will be a true revolution by making the expansion of that freedom a priority. But appealing as that might sound, it may not seem "for real."

If the future is accurately described by media reports as one of pension plans collapsing, government programs being cut back, and the cost of living soaring, doesn't that vision lack a basis in reality? Especially when these financial challenges will be coming at a time when "earned income" may have become just a memory for many older people.

Some days, there seem only clouds on the financial horizon for elders. Such as news that in the world's richest country, one out of ten Americans is living in poverty, many of them elders.

We are often warned that the trend line for elders is all down, down, down. In 1980, 50% of American workers had some pension coverage. But by 1993, only 40% did. In 1999, the median income of older Canadian families was only $26,400. And that isn't the end of the bad news.

When prophets tell us about the future of government programs, the sky can look darker still. For instance, some warn that the United States government's long-term unfunded liabilities for Social Security, Medicare, and Pharmacare may be US$51 trillion. So the future can look bleak for elders, especially the Boomers who are soon to become elders — the ones who enter their 60s in 2005.

But their future looks bleak only if we assume nothing else will change. That growing older must mean growing dependent, that there will be fewer young people in the 21st century to support the greater number of older people. So times will be hard for everyone. But the coming age revolution means we do not need to make that assumption.

Being older will not have to mean being poorer. Youthful vigor may be lost, but independence will not have to be lost with it. Doors of opportunity will open to older people ready to walk through them. One of them will lead to earned income from working for others. Another will show how older people can work for themselves. And the third will lead elders to making their money work for them.

ELDERS WILL WORK FOR OTHERS

An upheaval in the workplace is about to happen. Already the shift is taking place. The end of mandatory retirement is unavoidable partly because not all elders can retire with financial independence when they reach an arbitrarily selected age. Melrose Scott could not when he was told in 2004 that he had to leave his job with the New Brunswick Division of the Potash Corporation of Saskatchewan, because he had turned 65. On the job, he could earn $27.33 an hour and he wanted to stay on it until he could bring his pension up to a better level. But since the contract between the company and the union said 65 was the retiring age, out he had to go. Not a person to suffer foolishness gladly, he took his case to the New Brunswick Human Rights Commission on the grounds of age discrimination.

Will he seem an exception in the future?

According to a 1998 study by the AARP, 80% of Boomers expected to work after retiring from the jobs they were holding. By the time an anticipated 77 million Boomers in the United States reach retirement age in 2011, working in retirement may not seem the contradiction it once did. In the developed world, it will not be unusual for men and women to seek extra income, nor for employers to need them as workers.

This is why Barry Witkin had no trouble, at age 65, finding applicants when he published an on-line advertisement that he was about to open an employment agency for the 50-plus. He was not thrilled at the prospect of a work-free life for himself and hoped a sufficient number of other people would feel the same. He did not just hope for long. More than 3,000 enquirers e-mailed him back.

Are that many people hard up after age 50? Or 65? Working even part-time can make the difference between being a little short of money and having a little extra. So the future will see a shift from the "guillotine" definition of retirement, when at a fixed age, a knife comes down and chops your job off. It will be replaced by gradualism: working less than full-time but still enough to "top up" what a person is receiving from pensions and retirement savings. Retirement in the 21st century will be a process instead of an event.

Rather than moving from full-time work to full-time leisure, it will be common for people to hold jobs that are seasonal, or part-time, or have "flex-hours." Or maybe jobs that are do-able from home, when the worker wants to work. Each job will pay enough for elders to put some jam on the bread that their pensions have already paid for.

Should having to work this way bother people when the 20th-century ideal was full retirement on an indexed pension? According to a survey by Human Resources Canada, 82% of older workers prefer this kind of "phased retirement" as their way to maintain their standard of living. Already seven percent of early retirees (aged 55 to 64) had taken jobs.

In the United States, the prospects for elder employment are enough to justify an agency such as Senior Employment Resources in Annandale, Virginia. It serves job seekers over 50. According to its executive director, Susan Allen, the best market for them is in small businesses and non-profit agencies, for a mutually beneficial reason.

Small businesses and non-profits often have needs that are best filled by men and who women who do not want full-time work and do not need benefits, yet can still do quality work that Margo E. Schreiber, of the Illinois Department of Aging, says is "conscientious, dependable, and productive." But these will not be the only sources seeking older, "wannabe" workers in the 21st century.

Home Depot has already made an arrangement with AARP to recruit older people for some of the 35,000 positions it has to fill.

Other big employers have lines cast in the older workers' pool too, such as General Electric, Disney World, Days Inn, Travelers Group, Ralston Purina, and Radio Shack.

So many job opportunities will coincide with so many willing elders that by 2010 an estimated 26.5 million Americans aged 55 and over will hold jobs. Before this decade ends, one in five American workers will be over 55 years of age. Already conditions point to Canada following suit.

Like Social Security, the Canada Pension Plan does not penalize people for supplementing their retirement payments with earned income. So a return to work is already on. When the 21st century began, 20% of the income received in older Canadian households came from paid work. This was a turnaround, a harbinger for the coming age revolution. In the late 20th century, gaining leisure time was the priority for many. In the 21st, it will become a search for more income. As a result, having older people on the job will be as familiar a pattern as engaging women and minorities became in the 20th century.

Mandatory retirement will become extinct, a kind of economic artifact. In its place will come a phased, gradualist scaling down from full-time to part-time, from total commitment to partial involvement. That this revolution is already in its incipient stage is clear from a Statistics Canada report that the number of people aged 65 and over who were still on the job in 2001 was 20% more than in 1996.

So the Cassandras of the business media warn us that pensions will not be enough to live on? Or that pension funds may collapse? Or governments re-write the rules? The coming age revolution tells us: "Don't wring your hands over it. You can work for the extra you need. You can live as well as you ever did."

ELDERS WILL WORK FOR THEMSELVES

Working for themselves is something many think about during the years they work for somebody else. For various reasons they hold back. But the door of self-fulfillment can open when a person is older. Instead of being the end of the day, aging can mean it's morning again.

I found that myself when at 65, I took a pension obviously inadequate to support two people unless we cut back with a sharp knife — a very sharp knife. But why should we when I was still healthy? I could have tried for a job, but that would have denied us some of the freedom we thought we had earned. So I opted for a cascade of part-time jobs which, added together, could enable us to live very well.

I lectured one day a week for the college where I had been full-time; I served on the boards of three companies; I sat on a commission of the Canadian government; I wrote books; I wrote a column for a monthly magazine. None of them on its own gave us a living, but when put together on top of a small pension, we had almost enough. But "almost" is not "enough," so we moved in a direction totally new for us. We formed a company of our own, filling out the incorporation papers in the country kitchen that became our corporate headquarters for the next 10 years. A real family firm.

Our company, Stackhouse Consulting Inc. (with me as president and my wife as secretary-treasurer), did public affairs consulting for five years and then financial planning for another five. SCI did not make a fortune for us, or even a living. But it did what I am now writing about — it added enough to our other income that we did not have to do any of the things retirement counselors used to advise were inescapable. We did not scale down, nor cut back. We lived as well as we ever had without ever spending more than we were taking in. And this method helped with something just as financially prudent.

By earning enough income in this variety of ways, we did not have to draw on our RRSPs (Registered Retirement Savings Plans) until the regulations mandated we must. That meant we could accumulate — instead of spending — in a tax-deferred form of savings.

But wasn't that unusual? Something few others could try? No way. That is why I am writing in this personal fashion. Not to make extravagant, self-promoting claims — just the opposite. My purpose is to describe an option that can be tried by most people who have always worked for companies or institutions. The average older man or woman will be able to set up shop, and in doing so they can create their own jobs. Age discrimination will be no problem when they can hire themselves. It will be their part of the age revolution. And instead of this being a pipe dream about the future, it has already begun.

In the 21st century, we will see a new class of elders emerging, filled with men and women who see no reason why their reaching a certain age means they're out of the running. People like Peter Harrington, a man approaching 80, who insists on remaining the business activist he has been all his life. Peter says he still runs a business because his own personal "system" needs the stimulus that comes from having to face problems, make decisions, and cope with the "ups" and "downs" of business life every day. He could not stand living if there were no challenges in his life.

So Peter goes to the office each business day to manage Sarquhar International, the small but successful company he established some years ago to market dyes. Made in Britain, these dyes are distributed chiefly to theatrical companies, as well as to universities with design schools and to a few retail outlets. It is still a load for a man, in his 80th year, to carry. Yet it is not more than he can bear.

Busy as running his company keeps him, it does not provide enough dynamic for this entrepreneur. Peter is also into property management as the owner of two residences that he has subdivided into apartments. If and when the time comes that he can no longer cope with his dye company, Peter will still have these two buildings to look after, and to draw income from. He insists it will beat a retirement fund because it will give him the stimulus he needs as well as a steady income.

What this entrepreneur shows us is what studies confirm: Older people needing income can hire themselves. In Britain, a Barclays Bank survey reported that older people had opened 50% more businesses than elders had operated 10 years earlier. And most of them were doing it the way my wife and I did — not as their sole revenue source, but just as a way of adding to their other income. Only 27% used the business as their living, and for 51% it was an add-on to their pensions and other retirement funds. So the trend is there. And it will grow.

According to research at AARP, 80% of Americans expect to work after retirement, and of these, 17% look forward to operating their own businesses.

Research showed that the ratio of self-employed women aged 65 or more could be more than double that among women aged 25 to 54 years. Perhaps more impressive, the ratio of entrepreneurial women aged 65 or more was over 60% more than among women from 55 to 64. Will this trend maybe hold a time bomb waiting to bring the future down for older entrepreneurs?

Appealing as it may sound to the enterprising, some elders may be cautious about investing money and effort in something as risky as a new business. Reports of risk, however, may have been exaggerated. Brian Head, an economist at the United States Small Business Administration's Office of Advocacy, researched the record of small companies in the early 1990s and learned that about 65% of them were still active after four years. Of 5.5. million American business, not including one-person operations, only 10% went under each year. That was no guarantee of success, but equally no "red alert" warning us of failure. In fact, research shows that failure is more of a risk for younger people than older.

Elders have an advantage. Many have at least a house they can use as security for a loan. They may have been dealing with the same bank for years, and they have developed a credible credit record. They will usually undertake businesses in lines where they have had years of experience.

Older people thus can be one step ahead of their younger rivals when they can cash in their years of experience by offering what cannot be learned in a few years of academic training.

Starting up a business need not be a pipe dream. It can be a viable option for someone with a service or product to offer, someone who will need only part of an income to make life trouble-free financially.

For other elders, however, there's a better way still.

ELDERS WILL MAKE MONEY WORK FOR THEM

One of the most dynamic economic changes in the late 20th century was the popularization of investing. Instead of being the privilege of the few, it became an opportunity for the many. From being arcane knowledge held by an elite, it became a common interest of the majority.

In 1929, according to Joseph Kennedy, it was time for him to sell all his stock when he heard an elevator operator talking about shares he had bought. But by the end of the century, Joe could not have used that yardstick. Half the people in Canada and the United States owned — directly or indirectly — stock in one or more companies.

All of which heralds another dimension of the coming age revolution. A time when elders will support themselves — partially or wholly — from investments they own and manage themselves, or hold indirectly through mutual funds that someone else manages for them.

It will be an appealing way for elders to be in the money. It will demand almost no physical effort more strenuous than lifting a telephone to call a broker, or to switch on a computer, or to check on the latest market news offered all day long on television.

It will also be a great age equalizer because money in the hands of an elder is as useful as it is in the hands of a young hotshot. Age is no deterrent to managing money. Yes, an older person has to stay informed on what's happening, and to use judgment about selling as well as buying. But so does a young person. Age is not the priority. Just as college students can learn what makes markets rise and fall, their 21st-century grandparents will think no day complete without checking to see if the Dow, the TSX, or the NASDAQ was up or down.

So most pensions will not be indexed to keep pace with inflation? That will not have to threaten elders ready to supplement their retirement income with at least enough investment income to equal inflation, or more likely, go far beyond it. Instead of the market being the monopoly of eager, shouting, gesticulating young men and women on the "floor," the market will belong as much to elders scattered across the developed world.

One of them is already the world's leading investor, a septuagenarian who has become a financial legend in his own time. Warren Buffett (b. 1930) offers all elders a model for the coming age revolution. Not because many — if any — can achieve his success, but because he shows elders that they can be old and still make some money. Not as much as he does, but more than they would have if they had not made their money work for them.

Buffett is already past the age when people used to think it time to call it quits. But after making his first fortune, he tried retiring and learned it was not for him. So he returned to the investment arena and eventually developed his now world-famous Berkshire Fund. His method has been the simple formula of the first Baron Rothschild: "Buy cheap. Sell dear." Very simple. But in the hands of a master it can be brilliant. It has not only made him a billionaire, it has made money for all those who have bought into Berkshire, and it has also had an even more wide-reaching effect.

Buffett's fund has made the point that there's nothing intrinsic in aging that renders a person unfit to manage money. If there were, how would Buffett do what he's doing in his mid-70s? Or how would Federal Reserve Board Chair Alan Greenspan, also approaching 80, know what buttons to push to keep the economy from exploding or collapsing?

Yes, they are financial geniuses. True, most of us are not. But this is not an adequate answer. Not many older people can make the New York Yankees either, but many of them can still play ball with their grandchildren. They can also make their money work for them. Including those elders who will be risk-averse.

New options will emerge to help elders put their money to work for them. One of the most intriguing ideas may be investment clubs, where men and women pool resources, choose investments, and make profits that can be shared. Already there are so many clubs that there is a National Association of Investors Corporation based in the U.S.

To younger critics, that can seem just an example of greed gripping people when they should be focusing on spiritual priorities. But it will be the opposite. Not avarice but stewardship. Prudent money management will ensure 21st-century elders can pay for care, so that they need not be a burden on their adult children, or a fiscal challenge to a society faced with an escalating older population and declining youth numbers. Part of the coming age revolution will be the financial independence of a generation that — in earlier times — would have had to be carried.

* * *

Financial independence is essential to personal freedom. Age is no deterrent to this. Yes, an older person has to stay informed of what's happening, and to use judgment about selling as well as buying. But so does a young person. managing money is not the sole province of the young, as Warren Buffett clearly shows. In the 21st century, being old will not mean being dependant.

Chapter 7

Elders in Love

While training to be a marriage counselor, a university student asked a woman in her late 60s: "When does sexual desire start to weaken?"

The answer was revealing and also unexpected, because the woman smiled coyly, then replied: "I'll let you know."

It was more than quick wit, it revealed something unexpected about older men and women.

Sexuality does not take early retirement at 55, or late retirement at 75. Time does not erect a "fire wall" to keep romance from going one kiss further.

The Center for the Study of Aging and Human Development at Drake University claimed in the 1980s that four out of five men 60 years of age or more were still interested in sex. Should they not have been? Or should they have shared the assumptions of an ageist culture that, at their time of life, they should not even think about sex?

The time for that bias is past.

In the coming age revolution, sex will be too important to be left only to the young. Especially when the Boomers swell the elder ranks of the world.

Shaped by a culture that repudiated all inhibitions about sexuality when they were young, these soon-to-be-old men and women can see sex as normal a part of their lives in older age as it was in youth.

The coming age revolution will see becoming "neutered" by age for what it is: an anachronistic prejudice like those uninformed judgments about gender and race which were so firmly fixed in the culture just a half-century ago. But do we really have to wait for this to happen?

The age revolution's approach has already begun to give us all — youth and elder both — a new "take" on the love life of older people. Dr. Merryn Gott, of Sheffield University, reported that a survey of sexual activity among elders indicated it grew more satisfying with age. It also suggested that sexy elders may be healthier, physically and mentally, than their inactive contemporaries. But that should come as no surprise.

Three developing features of a new lifestyle among elders show sex, romance, and love are already becoming central to growing older in the 21st century.

One is the way pharmaceuticals are empowering middle-aged and older men with a sexual prowess which had so long been the privileged monopoly of youth.

A second change is elders seizing a new freedom to slip the bonds of their earlier lives. Perhaps to enter a new marriage. Or often, to bypass matrimony in favor of just living together. Perhaps not doing even that. Instead, keeping their own homes — or rooms in the same retirement community — but spending most days and evenings together.

Then there is a revolutionary desire to reclaim at least the appearance of lost youth. And that desire has now been put within the grasp of older people. Provided that they are ready to pay the price it demands — dieting, exercising, even surgery.

NO MANDATORY RETIREMENT FROM SEX

Pharmaceutical progress is making possible what previous generations could only dream of. Until just recently, the fire of desire might not have gone out. But for many, the flame of fulfillment could only flicker. Not any more.

For older men — and for many women too — Viagra became one of the great new facts of our time when it burst on an eager public in 1998. In its first two weeks of availability in the market, 36,809 prescriptions were issued in the United States. Until Viagra came on the market, the highest number for a new drug had been just 5,500.

One doctor — aware of the storm the announcement of this new drug could stir up — took the precaution of preparing a rubber signature stamp which could be put on his prescriptions. His foresight was justified. He issued 300 prescriptions himself on the very first day.

Nor did the public's interest wane after that initial spike. No fewer than 10,000 prescriptions a day were issued across the United States in the weeks that followed. And the desire to try the drug has yet to fade.

Especially when people learn of a 62-year-old who claimed he had had the hardest erection he had enjoyed in 40 months, one that lasted 45 minutes. He said he had not had such sex since he was 30 years of age. "It made me feel like a kid again," he boasted.

Another satisfied customer was a retired New York City firefighter who, in his 70s, still liked having sex several times a week. But his capacity for tumescence was not what it had been. And although his amours might be as frequent as ever, his satisfactions were not. Then Viagra entered his world. His love life became as good as it could get, and all because of a simple medication.

Whether enabled by Viagra or by one of the other pharmaceuticals (like Cialis and Levitra) that quickly came on the market, the desired erection results from increasing the flow of blood into the penis. This should happen naturally just by a man becoming sexually aroused. Nitric acid in the penis is then released. Next a chemical substance (guanosine monophosate) opens up the man's blood vessels. His penis is then hardened by the blood rushing into it. But life does not always proceed as it should.

For diverse reasons, this inflow can be stemmed by diabetes, by heart trouble, heavy smoking, damage to the nerves of the prostate, even from injections of female hormones to combat prostate cancer. Whatever be the cause, the result can be an inability to have an erection firm enough for a man to engage in intercourse. And he will then be labeled "impotent" because he no longer has the power to make coitus possible. The impact can be profound.

Can anything be more devastating to a man's self-image? It means the loss of something vital to masculinity. Along with growing a beard, it has been a distinguishing mark of passing from boyhood to manhood. To so many middle aged and older men, impotence means what one of them lamented: "Now I'm just half a man."

What else could he think about himself? Especially when the word for his condition was the psychologically debilitating term, "impotence." Still worse, when it was considered a life sentence.

Pharmaceuticals that could relieve the condition burst on the market as though they were miracle drugs. New medical marvels. Why not? They restored a dimension to a person's life and eliminated the debasing term "impotence," now replaced by the less threatening, less offensive, "erectile difficulty" (or to use the television commercial's euphemism, "ED"). So much did the whole subject become an accepted part of the culture that commercials could feature Senator Bob Dole, the 1996 Republican presidential candidate, as a spokesman. What could have saved men from their nervous inhibitions more than such a public figure talking to them man-to-man? What could better signal that they could now have great expectations?

It was nothing less than the start of a revolution. Everything could change. Where "impotence" had always sounded like the demise of virility, "ED" sounded like a problem that had found a solution. What man needed to feel threatened by the passage of time when his family doctor could write out a prescription that was like a ticket to renewed romance? An elder could be in love again. Fully.

Not only men are being affected by the new awareness that sexuality can actually last a lifetime, or at least a much more generous portion of it. Women, too, are part of the generation that entered puberty in the 1960s and 70s when so many inhibitions about sex were beginning to break down.

One 62-year-old woman says sex has never been better for her. Her children are grown and gone, she doesn't have to fear pregnancy, and since her husband is retired, she points out that the two of them can have sex any time of the day they want. "We can do it all day if we feel like it!" she laughs.

Are they unique, or prophets of an age revolution that will have an impact on the bedroom as well as the workplace?

Fitness programs and improved nutrition — as well as a more positive self-image — are already enabling women to ignore the passing of the years when it comes to being active, in both general and sexual terms. So the coming age revolution promises a whole new order in the romantic dimension of life.

And most people of both genders are looking for that change. What will be revolutionary will be that they take for granted the idea that older people should have a sex life.

In *The Starr-Werner Report on Sex and Sexuality in the Later Years* (1987), it was reported that of 800 respondents to a survey of men and women aged 60 to 91, 95% said they enjoyed sex. More impressive still was the report that 75% said sex felt better than it had when they were younger.

Part of the revolution is the ease with which older people will talk about sex. If many may still be inhibited from the conditioning of their youth, they will also feel some influence from the way their adult children — and grandchildren — are so much less "private" about all matters sexual. So they will enjoy a new freedom to venture outside the "reservation."

But like all social changes, this one may have its downside. Already the incidence of HIV/AIDS among older people in the developed, as well as the developing, world has been recognized. Like young people, they do not always practice "safe sex." Nor does their gray hair give them immunity to this modern plague. And the prospects are sobering.

According to the Center for Disease Control and Prevention in Atlanta, AIDS has increased five times among Americans over 50 years of age. It soared from 16,300 cases in 1995 to 90,600 in 2003. By 2004, older men and women were producing 14% of AIDS cases in the United States. Older women were 18% of the female cases.

How can this be? The Center for AIDS Prevention Studies at the University of California in San Francisco claims that elders are only one-sixth as likely to use condoms as younger people are. Older women also become more vulnerable than their younger "sisters" — not only because of physical changes, but also because they are less assertive in probing male partners about their sexual history and less demanding that men use condoms.

When liberty becomes license, to use the old maxim, danger can be even more prevalent among older people than younger. And unless what is already a pandemic in the developing world can be halted, the coming age revolution may threaten elders along with young people.

But sexual liberation is not the only prospect that can change the future for many elders.

RETREAD ROMANCE

Elder interest in loving will impact on the 21st century through increased separations and divorces, an escalation of elders cohabiting as well as remarrying, as well as seeking new relationships that do not involve living together.

The change has already begun. And right in the home itself.

Marriage breakdown is increasing among older people. Reports of an "epidemic" may have been exaggerated in some media accounts, but the fact that separation and divorce are becoming more "thinkable" among older couples is evident.

Prof. Andrew Cherlin, of Johns Hopkins University, Baltimore, says that although there may be no epidemic of elder divorces, older people are now more likely to choose this option than they would have a generation or two ago. The new feature is not that elders may be more prone than younger people to divorce, it is just that they are not significantly less prone.

Is this a spin-off from the dramatic upturn of marriage breakdowns across the world in the late 20th century? A development that transformed assumptions about "tying the knot" as a lifetime bonding for most people?

After "no fault" divorce legislation was introduced in Canada in 1985, divorces shot up 600%. In Russia, the number of divorces in 2002 exceeded the number of marriages in the first quarter of that year. They rose from four percent of marriages in the 1980s to 26% in 1995 in China, and spiraled up 40% in Switzerland during the years from 1980 to 1998, and a 75% divorce rate was reported in Cuba.

Is this true everywhere? In England, there has been a drop in the divorce rate from the 1993 peak of 180,000 to a lower 2001 level of 160,000. But either figure was several stories above the 1961 rate of 27,000. And significantly, the age of divorcees had risen from an average of 39 years for men to 42 years and among women, it had gone up from 36 years to 39. And those averages had to mean there were many people older than the average when they went into divorce court.

Across the world, the 21st century begins with marriage stability being a not-to-be-taken-for-granted prize. Even among men and women who — according to the mores of another era — are old enough "to know better." With a cultural change of that proportion, is it to be expected that this will not impact throughout the developed world's aging population too, especially when the Boomer generation has had such a reshaping influence on the social values of their elders as well as themselves?

In 2001 a survey of changed social attitudes among 673 men and women aged 56 to 75 reported that almost two-thirds had changed their opinions about homosexuality, abortion, premarital sex, and having children outside marriage. Contrary to the generally held presupposition that older people resist change more than younger people do, the study showed there was more thought movement among men and women over 55 years than under that age. It was a shift with major social ramifications for life in the 21st century's aging society.

If elders are more open to a different lifestyle for younger people, should it surprise us when they evolve one for themselves? Should it be beyond us to conceive of this evolution escalating even more?

In previous times and under different social circumstances, a man and a woman who had been united in matrimony for decades could usually be expected to stay that way. But — given the radical changes of recent years — can that be expected to continue unaltered?

A change like increased longevity can motivate people to look at a future their parents could not picture. If a man or woman reaches 65 now, they have a good chance of reaching 85. If that were not so — as in their grandparents' time — they might grit their teeth and tolerate the incompatible marriage they had endured since they were young. They could take solace in the gallows humor of an English aunt of mine who quipped in the face of adversity: "Cheer up. We'll soon be dead." But not if they must face another 20 years in an incompatible marriage, especially if other circumstances have changed.

A moral pressure, in previous generations, was to stay loyal because the mother of a man's children needed his income. Hadn't she been denied the chance to finance her older years the way he had? But with two-thirds of married women working outside the home in countries like the United States and Canada, that can seem an anachronism. Now an older wife may have her own pension and retirement savings, and they are not all the assets she can have to go it alone.

She may have developed her own romantic options too, or at least a whole constellation of relationships and interests outside the home. When an older husband and a wife add it all up, parting may not be the trauma it could have been for their parents.

Certainly not traumatic enough to prevent the number of divorced elders in the United States from reaching a total of 2.2 million, a one-generation leap of 34%. And of American men in their 60s, nine percent are divorced or separated — six percent more than those on their own as widowers. Had some of them split when they were younger and just stayed that way? Probably. But it is equally likely that for others, parting from their spouse was the long-delayed liberation they had been waiting years for.

Like the Oklahoma minister who divorced his wife after 49 years, just at the time they might have been planning their golden wedding celebration. For the wife, it was a heartbreak. For the man, it meant fulfilling his long-frustrated heart's desire. He claimed he had endured years of nagging, ill temper, and general emotional turmoil. He would not accept the prospect of spending the rest of his life that way.

But it is not always a case of the man staging the walkout. Two-thirds of American divorces involving people over age 40 are initiated by the wife. Adulteries outside the home or tyrannies within it might have been tolerated by more dependent women in a previous age, but part of the coming age revolution is manifest in women growing older with an independence that rejects their having to put up with the intolerable.

According to a survey reported by *AARP The Magazine,* 60% of single Americans aged 40 to 69 are women. Of them, most are single through having been divorced, as only 24% of single women in that age bracket had never been married.

But is this new propensity for marriage dissolution by elders something that can be found only in North America? Is it another sign of decadence the rest of the world is resisting?

No. In Japan, for example, comparable social factors have produced comparable results. Between 1973 and 1997, the number of husbands and wives who split after 30 years of marriage or more escalated from 820 to 7,609. Divorce at all ages multiplied in Japan in those years. But the greatest rate of increase was among elders. Some marriage counselors attributed it to an unforeseen negativity in retirement.

Where a Japanese man might have spent little time at home during his working years, retiring put him there day and night. What may have been an opportunity turned out to be a problem for many. It was claimed that some husbands and wives had never had a real conversation with each other during their years of going to work or raising children. Retirement meant finding that marriage notwithstanding, they were really strangers to one another.

Across the developed world, marriage stability among elders is no longer a universal feature. The 21st century begins with it becoming more probable than ever that older people — like younger people — will be on the lookout for partners with whom they can share their lives. And this can have unprecedented results.

In the past, being widowed often meant that an older woman could only look forward to a life on her own, as female longevity outpaced male survival. As a result, there were more older women around than men — too many for all to find mates even if they wanted them.

For decades, men's shorter life-span made widowhood the fate of most wives. When Britain's Queen Mother, Elizabeth, died, she had been a widow far longer than she had been wife and queen to George VI (1892–1952). No, that was not typical, but not unique either.

Now men are living longer, not as long as women, but longer than men did before. So some of this gender disparity will be moderated, with a romantic potential resulting: there will be more eligible husbands, and that can mean fewer long-term widows.

Some sociologists used to observe that women wanting husbands should move to northern communities with their large populations of single males. In the future, older women may not have to move at all to find a more encouraging selection of eligible men. Increased male longevity will improve the options right where they live.

Older women can now attract younger men as well as older ones. Through fitness, nutrition, and having a positive self-image, older women of the 21st century can seem younger than their grandmothers and great-grandmothers at the same age. They might marry a man of their own age, or they might marry a man who is younger. The revolution lies in their having freedom to choose.

If the trend toward marriage by elders is more likely to escalate than wane, it will not be without one alternative being considered. New trends also show how re-marriage is no longer the only approved option open to elders in love.

Living together out of wedlock became commonly accepted among young people from the 1960s and 1970s on. It is now growing as a socially acceptable alternative for elders too. The number of Canadians living together without being married now totals over two million, enough to make them the country's second largest city if they were hived together in one location.

In 2001, the Canadian census reported 1,158,400 couples cohabiting compared to just over 5.9 million married couples. The large majority were younger people, but was cohabiting confined to them? Not in the United States.

In the U.S., the 2000 census showed the number of cohabitating men and women aged 65 or over had doubled since the 1990 census. This number can be expected to increase dramatically by the next census because of another cultural factor: the Boomers. The Boomers are starting to enter the ranks of the elders, and are people who have never had to think there was something about cohabitation that meant "living in sin." It is estimated that as many as 40% of Americans now in their 40s have cohabited at some time or other. Are they likely to draw back from it as an option when they become elders?

According to the 2000 census, 964,000 cohabiting couples were aged 45 to 64. This is a growth of almost three times since 1990, and over four times what it was in 1980. Another 112,000 cohabiting couples were aged 65 or more.

What's behind this sea-change of values that makes living together no longer viewed as immoral, as "shacking up"? In a culture that esteems freedom of choice, it has become one of the options. Being divorced, for example, seldom brings the opprobrium now that it did a half-century ago when Queen Elizabeth II refused admission to the royal box at Ascot to statesman Anthony Eden because he had been divorced and remarried. Why would cohabiting now condemn a man or woman to automatic disgrace? Choice has become the absolute.

In any case, a pragmatic culture does not find it difficult to understand men or women choosing this option for reasons that have nothing to do with religion or morality. Just practical, everyday considerations.

Often people live together because marriage would demand too high a price. One Ontario private boys' school discovered that when the administration learned that the widow of a deceased teacher had invited her "boyfriend" to live with her. The arrangement with staff had been that a teacher could build a house on a lot within the school grounds and remain in it after retirement, though not if he took another job. In the case of his decease, his widow could continue in the house as long as she did not marry again — otherwise she would have to sell it to the school for use by another teacher.

But nobody had foreseen a widow cohabiting. The rules made no mention of it. So one widow did just that. She had her boyfriend move in with her. And there was nothing in the rules to stop this convenient arrangement. She was able to carry on with a secure roof over her head — and a man under that roof — as long she did not seek the erstwhile respectability of marriage. Cohabitation can help men and women escape other problems too.

A man or woman may be alarmed at marriage threatening a loss of health insurance or a survivor's pension to which a widow is entitled as long as she stays a widow. As well, cohabitation has other advantages. A man or woman who had had an unhappy marriage may prefer a less binding arrangement with a new companion. All he or she may want to do is share their lives in a happy, comfortable, commitment-free way. So why not just move in? They can get around to marriage later on if they want it. For now they can just enjoy each other. Since this no longer bears the social sanctions it did a little more than a generation ago, what's to stop two people now?

Clearly, religious or moral scruples may. In some cases, family pressure might. In a few, it may not fit with a person's professional obligations. But now that public disapproval has waned after a generation of young people living and loving "without benefit of clergy," it should surprise few when elders want to try it too.

How will elders find partners when time will have taken so many of their contemporaries? Will they not find themselves bereft of friends and acquaintances just at the time they suffer the loss of a spouse? Yes. But human nature is ever resourceful.

Twenty-first-century communications are already coming to the rescue of elders who are alone but do not want to be. In any city, newspapers can regularly carry advertisements like this:

A very loving, petite, fit, cute, 61-year-old woman who loves family, loves to cook, travel, hike and take long walks, is looking for a caring, romantic, family-oriented man . . .

Other ads tell us about agencies that will help a man or woman match up with someone compatible. Some show creativity by advising readers that three women would like three men (50–60) to join them for dinner. Or it could be martinis. A few are more venturesome. They advertise for married women who will meet married men for an evening of wining and dining. Newspapers no longer have a monopoly on this kind of search though.

The Internet has expanded the possibilities and accelerated them too. Agencies abound in cyberspace, all of them eager to meet any elder wanting help with arranging a date or a marriage. Many of them involve questionnaires that enable the agency to match up the applicant with suitable potential partners. Then can follow communication by email so that each person is free to learn something about the other before deciding to meet face to face. Does it work?

It works enough to keep these agencies in business. They depend solely on men and women being ready to pay for a service. Why should they not succeed when they can fill a need not easy for many people to satisfy? They are only a 21st-century equivalent to the marriage brokers that have been part of history. Almost any society needs some way to help men and women reach out to one another. Using high tech and mass media to do it is just part of adjusting an old need to a new technology.

Technology is imperative because the social scene has changed too radically for old methods of forming relationships to be adequate. There are too many middle-aged and older singles for everyone to rely exclusively on family and friends, churches and clubs. There are 34.5 million single persons aged 45 years or more in the United States — more than the total population of California or Canada. They are the most rapidly growing sector of the American population, according to Rich Gosse, chair of American Singles. This can be linked to a cultural factor.

So many live in large urban centers whose high-rise apartments and condos can be the most impersonal "villages" ever conceived. There are not the contact opportunities that are so available in smaller, more face-to-face communities. So what's a man or woman to do?

Some try online dating. It could not be more convenient since 70% of American seniors who own computers also use the Internet. Of AOL subscribers, 22% are aged 50 or more. According to an Ipsos-Reid poll, 60% of Canadians 55 or older had access to the Net in 2004, a great leap forward from only 48% the previous year. With that kind of online communication available, the time is ripe for elders seeking partners.

Can it be a surprise then that there are over 24 online dating services serving Americans who want to meet someone. Match.com reports a seniors' membership growth of 122% in one year. Seniors' Friend Finder, the largest service of this kind in the United States, has 1.4 million members. Comparable services are available to Canadians too.

What are they all looking for? Their objectives vary. Perhaps just a night out, maybe to see if a few dates can inspire a relationship, one that will lead to marriage or to cohabitating.

One thing is clear. The coming age revolution means radical changes in the way older men and women contact one another. The transformation is underway now.

The trend is advanced enough to support "speed dating" as a way of connecting people who have never seen each other before. In speed dating, several men and women are brought together, divided into pairs, and each pair is given six to nine minutes for conversation about themselves. Then each person is paired with someone else. At the end of the session, each person turns in the name or names of those he or she would be happy to have as a date. If two people choose each other, they are given contact information and can arrange to meet one another again. Is this a profit-making venture? Often it is. But community and church seniors' groups use it too. And their efforts cannot meet all the desires older people have.

SOMETIMES FRIENDSHIP CAN BE ENOUGH

Beechwood Place is a retirement community that combines a comfortable hominess with a touch of elegance. It suits Ruth Varty, now 93 but able to live on her own there. Especially since she developed a friendship with David Henderson, 87, who lives across the hall just one apartment away.

Their relationship began in much the same way as it might have if they were both in their 20s. Tea in the afternoon is one of the amenities at Beechwood. So Ruth took David a cup of tea when she noticed he had not come down for it.

Not long afterwards, he invited her into his apartment for tea after they had watched a movie downstairs. And so they became friends who have been "going steady" ever since.

Often they have breakfast or lunch in Ruth's apartment. They sit at the same table in the dining room for their evening meal. They go shopping for groceries at a market close enough for them to reach with the help of the walkers they both use.

Not only do they share their days and evenings, they share each other's families too. When one is invited out for dinner by a middle-aged son or daughter — or maybe an in-law or an adult grandchild — the other is included.

Even their churchgoing has been integrated. Presbyterian David joins Anglican Ruth when one of the regular church services is conducted at Beechwood.

"Since you spend so much of your lives together, have you ever thought of marriage?" Ruth was asked. "Oh, no," was the prompt but almost surprised answer. Implicit in those two short words was the query: "What would that add to what we have now?"

Two people making each other happy by filling what could otherwise be lonely days and evenings. That is enough for many who — for a whole range of negatives — do not want to marry, or even to move in with each other. They just want to share hours that are better when they are lived with someone else.

The range of negatives may include geography. Where Ruth and David live in the same part of the same building, two people — we can call Esther and Bruce — live a thousand miles apart. But somehow they are in almost daily touch with each other.

Although Esther had taken early retirement, she is on the national board of a volunteer organization. Its meetings bring her several times a year to the city where Bruce lives. He's now a widower and she's a divorcee. But they used to be co-workers. So it was easy for them to take up with each other when they just happened to meet during one of Esther's frequent fly-ins.

Between these visits, every six to eight weeks, the two of them make full use of all the communication that technology makes available. One of them telephones the other almost daily, they fax one another, they email, and they even send videos about themselves. The miles do not keep them apart any more than they want to be.

The fact is that neither is ready to give up their lifestyle. And they have found they don't need to. Others might. But they don't. So they are happy, doing their own thing, but also having someone with whom they can share themselves. And they do not need to be in the same space to do it.

The coming age revolution will show us more of that. More of people over 60 who have become boyfriend and girlfriend, maybe with sex in it, maybe without it. But definitely with something people need at any age.

Will the age revolution also open these opportunities to even more people?

PUTTING A NEW FACE ON AN OLD HEAD

Cosmetic surgery is coming into its own. Its popularity has been driven upwards unintentionally by ageism in the workplace. For a long time, aging people have dyed their hair or resorted to toupees lest they be rejected for hiring or promotion. But that is now no longer enough. People are turning to cosmetic surgery to give them the facial appearance that could ease their path at work. But they are not the first to use it.

Aging people were preceded into the cosmetic surgeon's clinic by others who had pioneered this part-art, part-science branch of surgery. According to one of its early practitioners in Toronto, women school teachers were the largest professional group who sought his services, and June was their favorite month for the procedure. The doctor reasoned teachers were paid well enough to afford it, and they had July and August to recuperate. By September's return to the classroom, the teacher might be older, but they would look younger.

Will the same motivations sustain the use of cosmetic surgery in the 21st century though? The question fits because the coming age revolution will remove much of the age discrimination people have suffered in the workplace. If growing older becomes the "in thing," why should people want to go through the pain and expense of cosmetic surgery?

It can be a matter of self-image. When older people develop a positive concept of themselves, it should not surprise anyone else that some will want to look like the pictures of themselves they have in their own minds. Especially when they look at people they know and see how different they look, and hear it's because they have had facelifts!

The surgery itself is not new. What will be revolutionary will be its mass appeal.

Surgery for the purpose of improving appearance is almost as old as civilization. Ancient Egypt held practitioners. India included physicians who could reconstruct the noses of women that had been nasally disfigured as punishment for committing adultery. In imperial Rome, freed slaves turned to surgeons who could remove all the marks of their former degradation. There is nothing new in the desire to be seen by others as people see themselves.

But there is something new in the advance of techniques and the affluence that is permitting a large market to evolve. There is something even newer in the common acceptance that men and women do not have to look as old as the calendar says they are.

The coming age revolution will expand that acceptance as part of breaking down the former lines of demarcation that so rigidly defined the lifestyle of people after they had passed a recognized time barrier. They were expected to "act their age," and look it too. Now that time barrier is being moved.

Not too long ago, cosmetic surgery was for people aged 60 or more. It is now sought by men and women in their 40s. Or even 30s — the age when some people are sensitive to changes that tell them their youth is more behind them than in front. So the coming age revolution can actually escalate the use of cosmetic surgery to give men and women — of almost any age — an appearance that fits how they see themselves as persons.

Some elders will want their jowls drawn back, the lines around their eyes and lips removed, wrinkles taken away from the forehead and the cheeks — all the wish list that once only movie stars and wealthy matrons could entertain.

Sprucing up one's appearance has always been part of taking an interest in romance. Whether male or female, a person wants to attract the other person by being attractive.

Upgrading one's wardrobe, having a new hairstyle, going for a facial, using only the best make-up. All these used to be thought part of being young, but for many elders, they will be part of having some love in their lives again.

Elders could once be expected to dress in black and view love from afar, but not in the future. In the coming age revolution, that time barrier just will not be there, nor will any impediment to romance that cosmetic surgery can remove.

Elders will not retreat from something that can add so much more appeal to their appearance. When people convince themselves that they have a future as real as their past, why will they want to look like men and women of yesterday, especially when this combination of science and art is available.

According to the American Society for Aesthetic Plastic Surgery, modified techniques now make surgery for older people not the "contradiction" it once was. Some effects of aging — such as in skin elasticity — still present challenge, but improvements in appearance can nonetheless be sought, and are being sought in growing numbers.

The Society reports that seven percent of procedures performed in 2000 were for men and women aged 65 and more. According to the American Society of Plastic Surgeons, Americans aged 65 and over accounted for 90,911 procedures in 1998. People aged 51 to 64 sought 242,427 procedures in that year. One-third of the procedures that year were performed for people over 50 years of age, especially procedures for rhinoplasty (nasal surgery). They were sought more by people between 50 and 70, but were not unknown among 80-year-olds. Should this development surprise us when elders are going beyond so many limits that were imposed on older people for so long?

As one surgeon put it, "more patients are having cosmetic surgery because they believe it is acceptable to want to enhance their appearance." And often that desire is linked to the return to romance that has become part of the scene for older people.

Openly admitted sexual interest, willingness to end marriages that are bane more than blessing, readiness to seek a second — or even a third — chance for happiness. All these are part of the coming age revolution. And with them, a desire to look the part, even if it means reshaping one's face in order to give one's life a new design.

According to one cosmetic surgeon, Dr. Paula Moynihan, in *Cosmetic Surgery for Women,* this surgery is more than an anatomical change. What she calls "image enhancement" involves a total development of the person so that what's inside matches what is being shown outside.

This is not achieved by pouring a psychological elixir into the person, but by enabling people to make the most of what they have — to use all their talents and traits which they may have been holding back because people think they look drab or they have been told their nose is too large. Cosmetic surgery can help remove this kind of barrier to personal confidence.

So an elder with a new romantic interest has a way of coping with an old psychological problem. The coming age revolution will see older men and women fulfilling desire instead of lamenting the loss of their youth. But physical changes will not be the only way open to them.

They will be helped all the more if they develop a new attitude to the world and their place in it, if they gain a personal philosophy that will empower them to feel at home in a new era for older people.

CHAPTER 8

A Philosophy for the Age Revolution

E very great revolution in history had been based on a philosophy. Before great changes can erupt, great thoughts must be conceived. Yes, revolutions have demanded people of action, but they have also been dependant on reflective thinkers to provide a language that can verbalize the passions of the revolution, to articulate its goals, to give a sense of direction, to advocate values to aim for. This may not satisfy many of us who are practice-oriented, results-driven, let's-get-on-with-it people. But even a glance at history can show how new ways of living have had to follow — not produce — new ways of thinking. A philosophy for the age revolution is needed now. It must be a foundation on which a new social order can stand securely. Just as most structures stand on four walls, this philosophy can be built on four central principles. Let's call them the four "V's": vitality, vocation, venture, and value.

VITALITY

Isn't this the last quality one would normally associate with age? We usually link vitality with energy, effervescence, enthusiasm, dynamism, speed. But these are not all that the word vitality means. Its root is the

Latin word for "life." It can remind us that while we are alive, we are still vital. We can also appreciate what the ancient Greeks said was imperative for people to be vital. They said it was having what they called a "soul." In the modern world, this word has often been given a religious meaning. But that is not what the Greeks had in mind when they spoke of our having souls. They meant it was the soul that empowered us to breathe and move. When death came and the body could no longer move, they said the soul had departed that person's body.

That bit of ancient lore may or may not interest us, but what does it have to do with aging in the 21st century? Quite a lot, as we can see if we reflect on one of the most remarkable documentary films of recent years: *The Fog of War.*

Its "star" — and almost its whole cast —takes the audience back to the 1960s. In 1961 when the newly elected president John F. Kennedy formed his cabinet, it contained so much talent that its members were called "the best and the brightest." Everyone was a star. But in that galaxy, none shone more brightly than Robert S. McNamara, the new secretary of defense. So mentally sharp that many called him "the computer," he had been an acute enough "number cruncher" to turn the Ford Motor Company around. Now he was ready to give up his corporate affluence so that he could pull the Pentagon together and make it work.

McNamara seemed made for the job, especially when organizing the escalating American involvement in Vietnam. But after a few years of using his expertise to manage the buildup in that war, McNamara underwent a kind of Damascus Road conversion. This apparently calculating, pragmatic action man turned on the war. He became convinced it was not winnable, and, even more, that the government could not justify compelling draftees to carry death to other people and risk death at their hands. This was unusual thinking at the Pentagon — unacceptable thinking at the White House. McNamara found himself unable to satisfy his conscience and hold his job. So out he went, a victim of Lyndon Johnson being traumatized by the prospect of losing a war on his presidential "watch." Now, more than three decades later, McNamara looks back on it all as he talks to his cinematic audience.

What makes it relevant to aging in the 21st century is the way this documentary shows how McNamara at 85 was the same McNamara he was at 45. Yes, he looked and sounded older, but he was still driven by the same combination of will and courage that had made him refuse to bow before the most obdurate and ruthless president the United States had ever had. A generation later, he was the same McNamara inside regardless of how he had changed outside. And that means something profound for the rest of us.

Aging does not have to alter us as souls no matter how it changes us as bodies. In each of us, there is a permanent identity, which denies that aging carries us past an invisible but ineradicable boundary to a different world called "old." Our having souls means we retain an essential character despite the passage of time. At 50, 60, or far beyond in time, we retain the essence of what we were when we were younger. The old oak may have been gnarled by time, yet it is still the oak tree. McNamara is still McNamara. Just as we still carry the names we received in infancy, so you and I are still what we were. We are human beings with souls.

What does that have to offer the age revolution? It should persuade us to abandon the assumption that at a certain age, men and women have to take on an identity defined by time, such as, "senior citizen," "retired," or "elderly." Such terms may be kindly meant, but they cannot avoid marginalizing human beings. The process is by implication but is not less real. Such terms erect psychological walls to distinguish and often separate people. They imply that to be older is to belong in the stands of the arena where one can only watch others run the race. They suggest a line that divides the meaningful, useful, participatory years from the less significant ones that follow.

That is why this ancient term — soul — can have a new importance. It can remind us that, to paraphrase the Bible, though the outward person is aging, the inward person is being renewed every day. The age revolution will declare that is still true. And nowhere more than in that area of life from which the 20th century tried so repeatedly to banish it: the workplace.

VOCATION

When my daughter Ruth was at New York's American Academy of Dramatic Arts, she fitted the description of a "struggling student." The training demanded total dedication, and the cost meant living on the edge. Yet she never wavered in her desire to stay and succeed. She was convinced — as she said in a letter to her father — "I am doing the work I was born to do. "

That sums up what "vocation" means. Its Latin root is the verb, "to call," and it should mean the work people believe is their calling in life. Often it has been limited to use by clergy, missionaries, and other spiritual workers claiming that God called them to their ministries, but it can be applied to any service by which people believe satisfies some human need. That can demand a revolution in our thinking because many people find it too big a stretch to apply terms like "vocation" or "calling" to truck drivers and stockbrokers, hair stylists and journalists. But the stretch was "doable" almost 500 years ago.

Martin Luther (1483–1546) turned the cultural assumptions of his time upside down when, as part of the Protestant Reformation, he claimed that the housewife in her kitchen and the carpenter in his workshop were fulfilling their vocations as much as the nun in her convent and the priest at his altar. By meeting the needs of other people, Luther taught, they were serving God's purpose on earth. They were working at their vocations as much as if they were working for the Church.

Apply that to older people now and we practice the message of some people who became prominent in England during the years following Luther. Called Puritans because they wanted to shape the Church of England "purely" according to their interpretation of the Bible, they claimed that vocation meant serving God in the daily round, the common task. But they also asserted that this meant a commitment of one's skills and strengths for life.

The 20th-century ideal of total retirement from work because a person has gained financial independence would have been alien to the Puritans. A person was urged to see work as a call to serve. A vocation had nothing to do with needing an income or being below retirement age.

One of the Puritans, Sir William Waller, wrote in his *Daily Directory*: "'What doth the Lord require of thee? Not to lie still. But to rise up and be doing." He recorded that he himself was up and doing by five o'clock in the morning during the summer and six in the winter. Puritan women understood their lives put this vocational demand on them too. Sir Thomas Wroth thus paid this tribute to his wife, Lady Margaret:

Neatness she highly prized, and hated sloth,
As did her words and actions all express.
She had no warrant — often would she say —
To spend a minute idle of a day.

Obviously that message does not appeal to anyone whose idea of heaven on earth is total freedom from work. But it can have an energizing effect on older people when they recognize that reaching a certain age does not have to mean retiring from their vocations in life.

It may mean giving up a particular job. It may mean stepping down from a leadership role. It may mean handing an enterprise over to someone younger. It does not have to mean turning one's back on the vocation that a person has always served.

Through the years my wife, Margaret, held several "jobs." School teacher. Museum teacher. Agency administrator. Company secretary-treasurer. But as she moved from one to another, she always practiced a vocation we can call "personal communicator."

Letters, cards, notes were written all over the world to a network of people we had come to know through students coming to our college or our visiting their countries. She has kept this vocation up so actively that our mail carrier once remarked to a neighbor, "Mrs. Stackhouse must know everyone in the world."

True, that's not a job. She makes no money from it, and she has no title, but it is still a service to let people know that someone has them in her mind and heart. It is doing what an old song urged us all to do:

Reach out and touch somebody's hand.
Make this world better if you can.

This fits one of my friends now in his 90th year, only he is still working at his vocation as a businessman. He started his company soon after returning from World War II service and has kept at it ever since. True, he has scaled down because he no longer travels across the land to advertise his wholesale jewelry to retail merchants. He relies on two sales representatives and an annual catalogue. The sales are small enough that he can package the orders himself in his own home. But he is still running a business. Still meeting needs. Still serving people. Still fulfilling his vocation.

In the 21st century, my friend will become less and less a rarity. And it will be a gain for everyone because life is fuller when it contains another quality that the Puritans demonstrated so long ago.

VENTURE

Unable to make the Church of England over in a Puritanized image, many Puritans left their homeland and crowded onto ships such as the *Mayflower* to cross the Atlantic in search of a place where they could form a "holy commonwealth." When they ran out of drinking water and beer within sight of land, they put ashore and called the place Plymouth after the Channel port from which they had sailed. The rest is history. But what history! What a venture! How could any of them have known they were starting the United States of America, or setting an example to future generations seeking justice and freedom?

Refusing to take risks or venture with anything brand new is usually seen as characteristic of older people. But there is nothing about growing older that demands a man or woman shrink from doing something new for the first time.

When Anna Mary Roberts discovered that arthritis was preventing her from doing the delicate embroidery work she had done for years, she could have folded her tortured hands, cursed her bad luck, and lamented that as a septuagenarian, she was too old to try anything else. Instead she took up painting, even though she had to use house paint for her first picture. But it was a venture that she enjoyed and others admired enough that an exhibition of her work was displayed in a drugstore window. An art collector passing by noticed the display, liked it, and promptly bought one of the paintings. It was the first sale this 80-year-old neophyte artist had ever made — but not the last.

As "Grandma Moses" she quickly gained a national and then a global reputation, which kept her painting until her death at 101. A phenomenal achievement which might not have happened if she had been convinced that when people are old, their venturing days are over.

Paul Helliwell was one of the most positive men I have ever known. Born to anything but affluence as a son of medical missionaries in

China, he was brought to Canada when his father came home to start a family practice in an Ontario village. But by the time he died as an octogenarian, Paul had made himself a wealthy man by never shrinking from a chance for a venture, even when he had passed what most people assumed was retirement age.

After returning from World War II service, Paul joined a Canadian bank, but in due course grabbed at the chance to venture on his own. He bought a small manufacturing plant in the Toronto area, grew the business, and then he sold it at a big capital gain. Before long he was ready to venture again, this time with a large milling company, which he made larger still until it was big enough for a friendly takeover very profitable to Paul.

Now wealthy enough to spend the rest of his life in well-earned leisure, Paul found that a permanent holiday was not his idea of a good time. So he bought a foundry at a good price because the industry was in decline and a recession had started. Neither negativity reduced his characteristic positive frame of mind, and soon the foundry was booming. Paul, now into his 70s, was having as much fun at the plant as he ever had sailing the boat that was his other passion.

But Paul ventured not only in business. He once remarked that his vocation was to make money and then give it away. Success in the second half of that vocation was as impressive as the first because Paul became a major benefactor of good works, both sacred and secular. When death came suddenly in his 80th year, he was still venturing in his dual vocation — making money and giving it away; living proof that there is nothing that says a person can't become bolder while growing older.

Every Sunday morning, millions of people around the world make a practice of listening to a septuagenarian who's doing just that. Not many men can start a ministry by preaching to 100 people and grow that congregation until it reaches an estimated 30 million, all who watch the Sunday services of the largest TV church in the world. Is that man a dynamic, charismatic young evangelist?

No, Robert Schuller is on his way to age 80 and serves still as senior pastor of the Crystal Cathedral in Garden Grove, California, not far south of Los Angeles. He started his church in 1955 with total assets of $500, which he used to rent a drive-in movie theatre where he invited people to worship while they remained in their cars and the minister conducted the service from the roof of the snack bar.

His people now fill a soaring glass edifice that cost $20 million to erect. It is the center for activities of all kinds seven days a week — conferences, seminars, concerts, tours. His church campus contains a day school, a book store, and a counseling center. All the funds for its multi-million dollar budget come from voluntary gifts. And the work of collecting support goes on relentlessly. With a load like that to carry, anyone nearing 80 could be excused for saying he had done enough and had earned a chance to rest. Not Robert Schuller. He goes from one venture to another, including having written 30 books.

True, not many people can play in the fourth quarter of life's game as adventurously as Grandma Moses, Paul Helliwell, and Robert Schuller. But not many could play that way when they were in the first and second quarters. There is nothing about age itself that must erase a venturing spirit from a person's soul. Anyone of us can use what we have regardless of our being young or old.

That's the message of one of the great epic poems of the 19th century, "Ulysses." Alfred Lord Tennyson (1809–92) pictured this mythical Greek hero confronting, in his old age, all the men who had crewed with him on the odyssey that took them to so many exciting places. Now Ulysses wants his old comrades to join him on one final voyage where they will sail to lands men and women have not seen. How can he ask them to follow him when they are now all so old? Ulysses acknowledges that time and fate have weakened them all. They are not what they were. But, he reminds them, "what we are, we are." It is enough for them to strive and not to yield. So he urges them to venture with him despite their ages:

Come, my friends,
Tis not too late for us to find a newer world.

Although elders are sometimes scoffed at for being no more exciting than a brown paper bag, many of them are extraordinary in their ability to find a place on the world scene. One of them, Maurice Strong, was doing in his mid-70s precisely what Ulysses was urging upon his comrades. After a phenomenally youthful business career — president of a major corporation at 35, and making himself financially independent in Canada's oil industry, Strong devoted himself to global crises that threaten humanity's future. Although never in political office, Strong held major United Nations appointments at the Stockholm and Rio De Janeiro "earth summits." He was also a driving force in organizing world relief for Ethiopia during the famine of the mid-1980s.

A senior advisor to the United Nations, Strong attempted to restructure its work in the interest of global governance. Not to create a world state, but to enable the UN to coordinate the world's efforts to give humanity a sustainable future.

Does this sound like venturing when a man was in his mid-70s? Anything that touches on national sovereignty can spark outrage in national governments, be they of a superpower like the United States, or a failed state like Zimbabwe. But Strong persisted in his cause. Age did not stop his traveling the world enough to justify four homes in four different countries. Challenge did not impede his persisting with the world's leaders to open their thinking to new possibilities. Like Ulysses, he remained sure it was not too late to seek a newer world. Not even for a septuagenarian.

This Ulysses-inspired spirit for venturing is all that older people need to transform the expectations they have for themselves. There is nothing inherent in age to prevent it happening. In this century, older people can enjoy a revolution of rising expectations, but to do it in the world at large will demand older people do it inside themselves with something that can only be inside.

VALUE

People at any age can live their lives to the full only if, to use Pope John Paul's words, "they count for something." And that has not been easy in a culture that has minimized the value of older people. Advertising has reflected a marketing prejudice that the important customer to be satisfied is under 50. Radio is often devoted to the latest youth fad regardless of older people comprising much of the potential audience. Clothing styles must be what young people will wear, or what those who want to "look young" will wear. In a culture like this one, how can older people think they count for something?

That is a crucial question because "value" is a relative term. A painting can be worth a million dollars to art lovers and look like junk to the people who clean the art gallery where it hangs. So too with people. We have value when we enjoy it in the eyes of someone else.

In the Bible the ancient Hebrew poet knew that when he prayed that God would make him as "the apple" of God's eye. He meant the image that stands in the center of a viewer's eye when someone is seen. So the poet prayed that God will value him so highly that God will always keep him at the center of his vision.

Was that conceit? Hubris? Arrogance? Or can we see it as the valid plea of a person who wanted to have value in the sight of another?

This prayer is relevant because it reminds us how most people do better when they can believe they are judged worthy in the eyes of other people, or do worse when they sense they are written off as "rejects." For a fully human existence, it is essential for a person to be accepted by others. So the coming age revolution will emphasize the imperative of changing the way old age is esteemed in our culture. And this can happen in the most paradoxical way.

Older people will gain greater value in the eyes of their society when they gain it in their own eyes. People who do not believe in themselves can scarcely persuade others to believe in them, and the first act of the age revolution will therefore be a reassessment of themselves and their place in the world by older people themselves.

The German philosopher, Friedrich Nietzche (1844–1900) challenged the culture of his time by calling for "a transvaluation of values." In the 21st century, the time has come for older people to do just that with their own self-conceptualization. No age revolution is possible without it, and no radical social change has ever been possible without "transvaluation."

A race revolution was possible in the 20th century only when African-Americans liberated themselves from the belief there was an inherent inferiority in their race. Symbolically they had to renounce the thinking of phrases like "black as sin" and "pure white." Then they had to replace them with a slogan such as "black is beautiful."

The race revolution needed legislation and court decrees. It needed protective armies and open education. But first it needed African-Americans to conceive themselves in a way denied their forbears.

The gender revolution required that kind of transvaluation too. Before equal rights laws could be effective, before closed doors of opportunity could be opened, women had to put out the garbage of dependency. They had to think differently about themselves.

In effect women had to see themselves through different glasses. As long as they wanted the deference of old-style etiquette and the assumption of male responsibility, they could not be free. A self-image change was imperative.

So too with older people today. A revolution can come only when older people refuse to sit on the sidelines or to be supported by younger people. Refuse to defer to the leadership of others, or expect special consideration because of age. Older men and women are doing unheard-of feats with mind and body. There is not the slightest shred of need for people to think age and dependence go together.

The story is told of a Hall of Fame baseball pitcher who was asked to play for a charity game. Its promoters knew that an appearance by this legend would excite a stadium full of his fans. And he did not disappoint them. In a token three-inning effort, he struck out several batters and did not allow a single run. When he walked to the dugout, the cheering was delirious. A young radio reporter remarked with a mix of surprise and awe: "He's been out for a lot of years. But he still has his fastball."

Every old person has some kind of fastball. Some talent. Some knowledge. Some quality that gives them unique value. Some way that person can count for something.

The aim of the age revolution is to make it count.

Bibliography

50 Plus (CARP). "Charlie Farquharson Unbuttoned." April 2004.

A/PACT. "Aging Parents and Adult Children Together." July 24, 2004.

AARP Public Policy Institute, "Boomers Approaching Midlife." *Journal of Gerontological Social Work,* Vol. 35, No. 1, 2001.

AARP. "The Facts About AARP's Position on Medicare Prescription Drug Legislation." December 1, 2003.

ABC News. "Splitsville At 71." August 25, 2004.

———. "Divorce Rate For Japan's Elderly Couples Is Growing." June 28, 2004.

Ackerman, Diane. *A Natural History of Love.* New York: Random House, 1994.

ADEAR (Alzheimer's Disease Education and Referral Center). "Alzheimer's Disease Fact Sheet." July 11, 2004.

ADWS.info. "Diabetes and Aging." July 11, 2004.

Ahmed, Kamal, Jo Revill, Gaby Hinsliff. "Official: Fat Epidemic Will Cut Life Expectancy." *The Observer,* November 9, 2003.

Alakbarov, Farid. "Nutrition For Longevity." *Azerbaijan International,* Autumn, 2000.

Aldrich, Marta W. "Many Seniors Delay Retirement." United Methodist News Service, December 29, 2003.

Allemang, John. "The Original Canadian Idol." *Globe and Mail,* August 23, 2003.

Allentuck, Andrew. "Widow Worries Assets Won't Last." *Globe and Mail,* October 25, 2003, C2.

Alphonso, Caroline. "Street Stalwart Marks 45 Years." *Globe and Mail,* September 14, 2002, B1.

American Society for Aesthetic Surgery. "Older Patients Benefit From Modified Cosmetic Plastic Surgery Techniques." September 7, 2004.

American Values.Org. David Blankenhorn and Tom Sylvester. "The Divorce Boom Among Seniors That Wasn't." *St.Louis Post Dispatch*, December 10, 2003.

Americans For Divorce Reform. "Correlations of Divorce Rates with Other Factors." June 28, 2004.

———. "Non-US Divorce Rates." August 28, 2004.

Andrew Scharlach, et al., "Who Is Providing Social Services to Today's Older Adults?" *Journal of Gerontological Social Work*, Vol. 38, No. 2, 2000, p. 6.

Arlett, Allen, Phelps Bell, and Robert W. Thompson. *Canada Gives*. Toronto: Canadian Centre for Philanthropy, 1988.

Assistant Secretary For Legislation, United States Department of Health and Human Services, Mark Rosenberg. "Testimony On Suicide Among Older Americans." July 30, 1996.

Atchley, Robert C. *Social Forces and Aging*. Belmont, California: Wadsworth 2000.

Bailey, Jeff. "Big Firms Can Share some Helpful Wisdom." *WJS Startup Journal*, December 28, 2003.

Bennett, Julie. "Ways To Finance Your First Franchise Purchase." *WJS Startup Journal*, December 28, 2003.

Biokhuis-Mulder, Jantie. "Is There Still Sex after fifty?" *Senior Living*, March 6, 2004.

———. "Seniors on the Dating Scene." *Senior Living*, March 6, 2004.

Blank, Joani, ed. *Still Doing It*. San Francisco: Down There Press, 2000.

Brown, John, ed. *The Sermons of Thomas Adams (The Shakespeare of Puritan Theologians)*. Cambridge University Press, 1909.

Carey, Elaine. "Aging Workforce Poses Real Challenge." *Toronto Star*, July 17, 2002, A1.

———, "Farewell to the Early Job Exit." *Toronto Star*, March 20, 2001.

Carter, Jimmy. *The Virtues of Aging.* New York: The Library of Contemporary Thought, 1998.

Chambers, Carl D., et al. *The Elderly.* Athens, Ohio: Ohio University Press, 1987.

Chen, Yung-Ping, and John C. Scott. "Gradual Retirement." *North American Actuarial Journal*, July 2003.

Cheney, Peter. "They'll Bop Till They Drop." *Globe and Mail*, February 28, 2004, F4.

Clark, Margaret and Anderson, Barbara Gallatin. *Culture and Aging.* Springfield, Illinois: Charles C. Thomas, 1967.

Cliffe, J. T. *The Puritan Gentry.* London: Routledge and Kegan Paul, 1984.

CNEWS Features. "Older Women Ask Unfaithful Spouses For Divorce." June 28, 2004.

CNews Home. "Older Folks Get Hip." April 18, 2001.

Cole, Thomas R., and Mary G.Winkler. *The Oxford Book of Aging.* Oxford: Oxford University Press, 1994.

Cornwell, Rupert. "Stop the Madness." *Globe and Mail*, July 6, 2002.

Costa, Dora, *The Evolution of Retirement.* Chicago: University of Chicago Press, 1998.

Csikai, Ellen L. and Ameda A. Maretta. "Preventing Unnecessary Deaths." *Journal of Gerontological Social Work*, Vol. 38, No. 3 2002.

DeBergo, Paige. "Vision of the Future." *Health Journal*, Spring 2001.

Deets, Sara Munson, and Leaker, Lagrette Tallent. *Aging and Identity.* Westport, Connecticut: Praeger, 1999.

Desjardins, Bertrand. *Population, Ageing and the Elderly.* Ottawa: Statistics Canada, 1986.

Divorce Magazine.Com. "Swingin' Seniors." April 9, 2001.

Dixon, Guy. "Achiever Keeps Firing on All Cylinders." *Globe and Mail*, June 12, 2002, C1.

Doegernomes.Org. "About the Human Genome Project." December 15, 2003.

Drohan, Madelaine. "Retirement Age Must Be Raised." *Globe and Mail,* August 4, 2000, B8.

Drucker, Peter. *Toward the Next Economics and Other Essays.* New York: Harper & Row, 1981.

Dychtwald, Ken, and Flower, Joe. *The Age Wave.* Los Angeles: Jeremy Tarcher, 1989.

Edelman, Deborah. *Sex in the Golden Years.* New York: Donald J. Fine, 1992.

Eesti Pereplaneerimise Liit. "HIV/AIDS Cases Rising Among Older Women." March 18, 2004.

Elder Jobs.Com. "Job Seekers." July 11, 2004.

Ellis, Michael. "Gilmour Returns to Become Ford's CFO." *Globe and Mail,* May 21, 2002, B12.

Erasmus. "The Old Men's Chat" and "The Carnage" from *Colloquies.*

Family Facts.Ca. "Cohabitation Among Canadians."

Fields, Robin. "Seniors Pick Cohabitation Rather Than Marriage." *Los Angeles Times,* September 4, 2001.

Fosdick, Raymond B. *The Story of the Rockefeller Foundation.* New York: Harper and Brothers, 1957.

Freedman, Marc. *Prime Time.* New York: Public Affairs, 1999.

Fried, Stephen, Dorothy Van Booven, and Cindy MacQuarrie. *Older Childhood.* Baltimore: Health Professions Press.

Friedan, Betty. *The Fountain of Age.* New York: Simon & Schuster, 1993.

———. *The Feminine Mystique.* New York: Dell, 1964.

Friedman, Milton. *Free to Choose.* New York: Avon, 1980.

Galloway, Gloria. "Mandatory Retirement." *Globe and Mail,* December 26, 2003, A11.

Galt, Virginia. "CEOs Urged To ëGet A Life' Now, *Globe and Mail,* November 28, 2002, BI.

———. "More Firms offering Flex-Time Option." *Globe and Mail,* August II, 2003, BI.

———. "Phased Retirement." *Globe and Mail,* June 23, 2001.

———. "Retirees Increasingly Keen to Return to Work." *Globe and Mail,* Jan. 30, 2004, BI.

Geriatrics, vol. 55, no. 10, October 2000.

Gifford, C. G. *Canada's Fighting Seniors.* Toronto: James Lorimer. 1990.

Globe and Mail. "Not Tonight Dear, I'm On Viagra." October 25, 2003, F7.

Go 60.Com. "Let's Go Dispel Some Ageing Myths." September 10, 2001.

Goldberg, Robert, and Gerald Jay Goldberg. *Citizen Turner.* New York: Harcourt Brace, 1995.

Golfonline. "Jack Nicklaus." December 10, 2003.

Graebner, William. *A History of Retirement.* New Haven: Yale University Press, 1979.

Gray Panthers. "Selected Achievements: 1970–2002." December 1, 2003.

Guillemard, Anne-Marie. *Aging and the Welfare State Crisis.* Newark: University of Delaware Press, 2000.

Ha, Frank B., Jo Ann E. Manson. Meir J. Stampfer, Graham Colditz, Simon, Liu, Caren G. Solomon, Walter Willett. "Diet, Lifestyle and the Risk of Type 2 Diabetes Mellitis in Women." *New England Journal of Medicine,* vol. 345, no. II, September 13, 2001.

Hamilton, Michael S. "We're In The Money!" *Christianity Today,* September 12. 2001.

Hampson, Sarah. "All In The Family." *Globe and Mail,* May II, 2000, R3.

Havens John J. and Paul G. Schervish. "Millionaires and the Millenium: New Estimates of the Forthcoming Wealth Transfer and the Prospects for a Golden Age of Philanthropy." Boston College Social Welfare Research Institute, October 19, 1999.

Health Canada. "Canada's Seniors, No. 1 - A Growing Population." July 24, 2004.

———. "Canada's Seniors, No. 2 - Canada's Oldest Seniors." July 24, 2004.

Hill, Gerry B. et al. "Life Expectancy and Dementia in Canada." *Chronic Disease In Canada,* Vol. 18, No. 4, 1997.

HSC Communications. "Study Reveals Older Parents Value Their Adult Children Living with Them." July 24, 2004.

Huddleston, Cameron. "Land the Job You Want." Kiplinger.Com, October 23, 2003.

Ibbitson, John. "Birth rate and population decline." *Globe and Mail,* March 2, 2002.

iBerkshire.Com, "Ask The Senator." December 10, 2003.

Immen, Wallace. "MD Blazed A Trail." *Globe and Mail,* February 22, 2002, A21.

Jayne Fisher, "Rekindle the Flames of Romance." August 25, 2004.

Jennings, Rob. "Fleet Empire State Building Run-Up." NYRR On Line, December 10, 2003.

Johnson, Julia, and Robert Slater. *Ageing and Later Life.* London: SAGE, 1993.

Johnson, Paul, and Pat Thane. *Old Age from Antiquity to Post Modernity.* London and New York: Routledge, 1998.

Jonathan Barry Forman and Patricia L. Scahill. "Issues for Implementing Phased Retirement In Defined Benefit Plans. "

Kahn Albert E. *Joys and Sorrows.* New York: Simon & Schuster, 1974.

Kamai, Ahmed. "Britain to Scrap Retirement Age." *The Observer,* May 12, 2002.

Kanin, Garson. *It Takes a Long Time to Become Young.* Boston: G.K.Hall, 1978.

Keck, David. *Forgeting Whose We Were.* Nashville: Abingdon, 1996.

Kerr, Ann. "Workers Spurn Retiremnt." *Globe and Mail,* February 18, 2002, C1.

Kimberly A. Henry, M.D. with Maria Costa. *The Face-Lift Sourcebook.* Los Angeles: Lowell House, 2000.

Knechtel, Robert. "Productive Aging in the 21st Century." *Employment of Seniors,* November 10, 2003.

Knowlton, Leslie. "Treating Suicidal Elders." *Geriatric Times,* 2003.

Kosberg, Jordan and Leonard W. Kaye, eds. *Elderly Men.* New York: Springer, 1997.

Kropf, Nancy P. "Strategies To Increase Student Interest in Aging." *Journal of Gerontological Social Work,* Vol 39, No. 1/2, 2002.

Kuitenbrower, Peter. "Barber's Chair Empty After 52 Years." *National Post.*

Las Vegas Review-Journal. "Seniors and the Stock Market Decline." July 28. 2002.

Laslett, Peter, A Fresh Map of Life. London: Weidenfeld and Nicolson, 1986.

Lehner, Maria. "Dating in the Gray Zone." Fox News.Com, February 25, 2005.

Levin, Jack, and William C. Levin. Ageism, *Prejudice and Discrimination against the Elderly.* Belmont, California: Wadsworth, 1980.

Lewington, Jennifer. "Canada Facing Age Crunch." *Globe and Mail,* July 17, 2002.

Lief, Clifton. "Why We're Losing the War on Cancer." *Fortune,* March 22, 2004.

Lovas, Carl. "Older Executives Can Give Employees A New Lease of Life. "

Lu, Vanessa. "Doctors Who Care for the Elderly." *Toronto Star,* March 20, 2001.

Lunman, Kim. "Seniors Staying At Work Longer." *Globe and Mail,* February 26, 2004, A11.

MacDonald, Gayle. "Walter's War On Bush." *Globe and Mail,* December 15, 2001, R7.

Mackie, Richard. "Official Attacks Mandatory Retirement." *Globe and Mail,* June 14, 2002, A10.

Mamashealth.com. "Coronary." July 11, 2004.

———. "Strokes—Major Health Concern of Aging." July 11, 2004.

Marriage Builders. "Married Life After Retirement." March 1, 2004.

Marron, Kevin. "Lines Between Work, Retirement Blur." *Globe and Mail,* May 11, 2000, B28.

McCallum, Mary. "Senior Sense: Senior Dating, It's Never Too Late." *Council On Aging In Southeastern Vermont,* August 25, 2004.

McCarthy, Shawn. "Shortage of Workers." *Globe and Mail,* September 7, 2001, A1.

McKendrick, Paul. *The Philosophical Book of Cicero.* New York: St. Martin's Press. 1989.

McLuhan, Marshall. *The Medium and The Light.* Toronto: Stoddart, 2000.

Meier-Ruge, W., ed. *Dementing Brain Disease in Old Age.* Basel: Karger, 1993.

Michael, Robert T., John H. Gagnon, Edward O.Lauman, Gina Kolata. *Sex In America.* Boston: Little Brown, 1994.

Mitchell, Allison. "Life Expectancy in Canada." *Globe and Mail,* September 225, 2003.

Mitchell, Andy. "Public Pensions: 75 Years of Helping Canadians." *Muskoka Advance,* August 25, 2002.

Mittelstaedt, Martin. "Sir Edmund Isn't About To Slow Down." *Globe and Mail,* Nov. 7, 2003, A6.

Modern History Sourcebook. "Andrew Carnegie: The Gospel of Wealth, 1889." August1997.

Monk, Abraham, ed. *The Columbia Retirement Handbook.* New York: Columbia University Press, 1994.

Morentaler, Abraham. *The Viagra Myth.* San Francisco: Jossey Bass, 2003.

Morris, Charles R. *The AARP.* New York: TIME Books, 1996.

Moses, Barbara. "Plan Ahead To Beat Retirement Blues." *Globe and Mail,* April 3, 2002, C1.

——. "Slowing Pains Flare Up." *Globe and Mail,* April 1, 2002, B16.

——. "Workers Ride Out Career Doldrums." *Globe and Mail,* January 7, 2002, C1.

Moynihan, Paula. *Dr. Paula Moynihan's Cosmetic Surgery for Women.* New York: Crown, 1988.

MSNBC. "U.S. Life Expectancy Hits New High." September 13, 2002.

Muggeridge, Malcolm. *Something Beautiful for God.* London: Collins, 1971.

Muhtada, Luma. "Working In A Golden Age." *Globe and Mail,* July 10, 2003.

New York Times, Editorial. "A Victory For Gay Marriage." November 20, 200.

The News Journal. "Reheboth Charging For Handicapped Parking." July 24, 2004.

NIMH. "Older Adults: Depression and Suicide Facts." December 16, 2003.

Norwell. Iris. *Women Who Give Away Millions.* Toronto: Hounslow, 1996.

Oberman, Mira. "Tenured Posts Among Budget Casualties." *Globe and Mail,* June 21, 2002, C3.

The Observer. "Why The Old Are On The March." August 1, 2004.

Ohio State University. "Elderly Less Likely than Other Adults to Have Economic Problems." March 1, 2004.

Ontario Human Rights Commission. *Time for Action: Advancing Human Rights for Older Ontarians.* Toronto: OHRC, 2001.

Ostrower, Francis. *Why the Wealthy Give.* Princeton, NJ: Princeton University Press, 1995.

Ozawa, Martha N. and Young Choi. "The Relationship Between Pre-Retirement Earnings and Health Status in Old Age." *Journal of Gerontological Social Work,* Vol. 38, No. 2, 2000, p. 19.

Palmer Course Design. "Arnold Palmer: A Biography." December 10, 2003.

Peritz, I. "Granny, Grandpa Surfers Riding the Web Wave." *Globe and Mail,* Sept. 21. 2004, A3.

Personal Surgeon Library. "Who's Having Cosmetic Surgery?" November 17. 2000.

———. "Rhinoplasty Among Older Patients." November 15, 2000.

Peterson, Peter G. *Gray Dawn.* New York: Times Books, Random House, 1999.

Pew Forum. "Part 2: Gay Marriage."

Phillips, David R. *Ageing in the Asia Pacific Region.* London: Routledge, 2000.

Phillipson, Chris and Alan Walker. *Ageing and Social Policy.* Aldershot, UK: Gower, 1986.

Picard, A. "Role of Grandmothers Crucial for Tree of Life." *Globe and Mail,* March 11,2004, A3.

Picckler, Nedra. "How To Work Till You're 100." *Globe and Mail,* December 24, 2001, B7.

Plaut, W. Gunther. *The Price and Privilege of Growing Old.* New York: CCAR Press, 2000.

Posner, Michael. "King of the Producers." *Globe and Mail,* July 19, 2003, R9.

Posner, Richard A. *Aging and Old Age.* Chicago: University of Chicago: 1995.

Price, Deb. "Gay Marriage Rights." *Desert Sun,* February 10, 2004.

Rajam, S. I. "Home Away From Home." *Journal of Housing for the Elderly* Vol. 16, No. 1/2, 2002.

Rees, Thomas D., with Sylvia Simmons. Toronto: Little, Brown, 1987.

Reid, Dixie. "Terkel's Circle." December 28, 2001, R5.

Reiss, Madeleine. "The Golden Years." Village.co.uk., August 25, 2004.

Research At Boston University. "The Secrets of Centenarians." December 10, 2003.

Retirement Planner. "Working After Retirement." January 6, 2003.

Rist, J. M. *Stoic Philosophy.* Cambridge, 1969.

Rose Dobrof, "From The Editor." *Journal of Gerontological Social Work,* Vol. 35, No. 2, 2001.

Rosene, Lou A., Julia E. Malphus, L.J.Dragore, Donna Cohen. "A Comparison of Characteristics of Kevorkian Euthanasia Cases and Physician Assisted Suicides in Oregon." *The Gerontologist,* vol. 41. no. 4, 2001.

Ross, Alec. "Retirees See Promise in Self-Employment." *Globe and Mail,* October 1, 2001, B8.

Rozzack, Theodore. *America the Wise.* Boston: Houghton Mifflin, 1998.

Ruane, Christine. "Poverty Is Not A Vice." *Journal of Social History,* Spring 1998.

Ryken, Leland. *Worldly Saints: The Puritans as They Really Were.* Grand Rapids, Michigan: Academic Books, Zondervan, 1986.

Sakurai, Joji. "Divorce Rate for Japan's Elderly Couples is Growing." Associated Press, August 25, 2004.

Sandra Block. "Tax Regulations Frustrate Many Workers." *USA Today,* November 29, 2002, B1.

Schachter, Harvey. "How Warren Buffett Fares as a Manager." *Globe and Mail,* Dec. 26, 2001, B7.

Schetagne, Sylvain. "Health Care Tops Seniors' Concerns." Columbia Foundation.

Schick, Frank L., and Renee Schick, eds. *Statistical Handbook on Aging Americans*. Phoenix, Ariz.: Onyx Press, 1994.

Scott, Paula. *Growing Old in the Early Republic*. New York: Garland 1997.

Secunda, Victoria. *By Youth Possessed: The Devil of Age in America*. Indianapolis: Bobbs Merrill, 1984.

Senior Friend Finder. "Divorce Rates in the United States." August 24, 2004.

Senior Journal.Com. "AARP Sponsors First-Ever Triathlon." December 12, 2003.

——. "Kemper Funds Reveal Investors Over Age 55 Control Nation's Wealth." December 28, 2003.

Senior Net. "Research On Senior's Computerand Internet Usage, 1998." Feb. 12, 2003.

Serow, William J., David F. Sly, J. Michael Wrigley. *Population Aging in the United States*. New York: Greenwood, 1990.

Simpson, Eilean. *Late Love*. New York: Houghton Mifflin, 1994.

Simpson, Jeffrey. "Why Our Provinces Are Running Scared." *Globe and Mail,* Nov. 8, 2003, A27.

Snowden, David. *Aging with Grace*. New York: Bantam Books.

Stones, Lee, and Michael Stones. *Sex May Be Wasted on the Young*. North York: Captus Press, 1996.

Sutherland, Jim. "Jimmy Has The Last Laugh." *Report On Business Magazine, The Globe and Mail,* April 2004, P.38.

Taber, Jane. "A New Career Beckons Elder Statesman." *Globe and Mail,* October 14, 2003, A4.

Taeuber, Cynthia M. *Statistical Handbook on Women in America*. Phoenix, Arizona: NYX Press, 1996.

Tallis, Raymond. *Increasing Longevity*. London: Royal College of Physicians of London, 1998.

Tanzi, Rudolph E., and Ann B. Parson. *Decoding Darkness*. Cambridge:

Perseus, 2000.

Terkel, Studs. *Coming of Age.* New York: New Press, 1995.

Terry, Sara. "Older Women's Newer Models: Gray Is Glam." *Christian Science Monitor,* June 09, 2000.

Texas Straight Talk. "Privatization' of Social Security Poses Risk." Oct. 2, 2000.

Thane, Pat. *Old Age in English History.* Oxford, 2000.

Thorburn, May, and Suzy Powling. *The Relate Guide to Loving in Later Life.* London: Vermilion, 2000.

Time Magazine, October 20, 1997; May 4, 1998, May 24, 1999; May 24, 1999; February 14, 2000; June 12, 2000.

Vincent, John, Guy Patterson, Karen Wale. *Politics and Old Age.* Aldershot, UK: Ashgate, 2001.

Wagner, John A., Eugene P. Falk, Barry J. B.White. *Nose Refinement.* London: J.B.Media, 1991.

Wallach, Joel, and Ma Lin. Rare Earths Forbidden Cures.

Walton, Dawn. "Retirees Returning to the Work Force." *Globe and Mail,* September 27, 2002, A8.

Warson, Albert. "Developer Shipp Feted." *Globe and Mail,* February 10, 2004, B10.

———. "Walter Zwig A Lifetime Achiever." *Globe and Mail,* February 12, 2002.

West, Michael. "Cloning Research Paying off, Texan Says." *Globe and Mail,* December 1, 2001.

Willis, Andrew. "Forget Freedom At 55." *Globe and Mail,* April 11, 2002, A1.

Wise, David A. Facing The Age Wave.

Wister, Andrew and Glona Gutman, "Housing For The Elderly." *Journal of Housing for the Elderly,* Vol. 12. No. 1/2, 1997.

Woodhouse, A.S.P., ed. *Puritanism and Liberty.* Chicago: University of Chicago Press, 1950.

Wykle, May. L. and Amasa B. Ford, eds. *Serving Minority Elders in the 21st Century*. New York: Springer, 1999.

Yalom, Marilyn. *A History of the Wife*. New York: HarperCollins, 2001.

Yung-Ping Chen and John C. Scott, "Gradual Retirement: An Additional Option in Work and Retirement." (actuarial)

Zarcone, Carmela. "Building Bridges Across Generations in the Workforce." *The Telegraph of Nashua, NH,* January 24, 2000.

Zaslow, Jeffrey. "Will You Still Love Me When I'm...84." WSJ: Career Journal.Com, March 1, 2004.